American National Government and Public Policy

Randall B. Ripley

 THE FREE PRESS
A Division of Macmillan Publishing Co., Inc.
NEW YORK

Collier Macmillan Publishers
LONDON

The Free Press
A Division of Macmillan Publishing Co., Inc.
866 Third Avenue, New York, N.Y. 10022

Collier–Macmillan Canada Ltd.

Library of Congress Catalog Card Number: 73–10574

Printed in the United States of America

Printing number

1　2　3　4　5　6　7　8　9　10

Library of Congress Cataloging in Publication Data

Ripley, Randall B
　　American National Government and public policy.

　　Includes bibliographical references.
　　1.　United States--Politics and government--
Handbooks, manuals, etc.　I.　Title.
JK274.R7　　　　　320.4'73　　　　　73-10574
ISBN 0-02-926540-1

To M.S. and S.C., for sustenance

Contents

v

Preface

This book focuses on the institutions of the American national government and the environment in which they are set. It is particularly concerned with the way those institutions work to produce public policy. An introductory chapter offers a general overview of the nature of the government and the nature of policy making. The next four chapters focus on various aspects of the political setting in which the government works: public opinion, political parties, voting and elections, and interest groups. The four chapters following those describe and analyze the functioning of the principal federal institutions: the presidency, the bureaucracy, Congress, and the courts. A final chapter offers some explanations of policy-making variations and addresses the question of governmental responsiveness to public needs.

Although the book is relatively brief, I have sought to deal with the major topics of which anyone interested in a serious introduction to the American national government as a policy maker should be aware. In dealing with these topics I have followed several practices quite consistently:

1. I have not attempted to be encyclopedic on any topic. All of the important topics needed for a thorough study of each subject are present, but their treatment is selective.

2. The focus is on contemporary American government. American political history is rich and well worth detailed study, and I firmly believe that political scientists should be well grounded in the history of the institutions and processes they study. In order to keep my presentation at a reasonable length, however, history has been largely ignored.

3. This book is based on empirical evidence, not on emotion or ideology. Polemics make good reading if they are well done, but they contribute little to a balanced introductory understanding of our government. Attacks or defenses of the government are appropriate and useful, but to have validity they must be based on empirically supported analysis. Some books give students arguments and no facts. This book seeks to give students facts and interpretations as the basis for a variety of arguments they can then construct for themselves or with the aid of their teachers.

4. The stress on analysis means that considerable data will be presented. In some cases they will be presented in tabular form; in some cases in verbal form. In no cases will they be presented in an esoteric, jargon-ridden, or hard-to-understand form. It is assumed that a serious student will learn how to interpret data, but there is no attempt to overwhelm the student with either too many data or data presented in arcane ways.

My hope is that this volume will find use as a basic text in at least three different kinds of undergraduate courses: (1) general introductions to American government, (2) introductions to public policy, and (3) beginning comparative government courses that include the United States.

A student who pays careful attention to what follows should come away with a good sense of the structure of American national government, the political environment in which that government operates, and the public policy that government makes. With such an underpinning he or she can then become a more intelligent critic or defender of "the system." Even more important, he or she can become a more intelligent participant in the political life of the nation.

R.B.R.

Acknowledgments

I am indebted to my faculty colleagues in the Department of Political Science at Ohio State University for interacting with me on a number of ideas presented herein and to my students in courses on American national government, the legislative process, the presidency, and public policy for doing the same thing. The staffs of the Ohio State Instruction and Research Computer Center and the Polimetrics Laboratory of the Department of Political Science were helpful in the presentation of data in Chapters 3 and 4, as was my friend and colleague, William Moreland. Finally, I am grateful to my friend and colleague, Grace Franklin, for her imaginative assistance at every phase of the preparation of this text.

PART 1

The Policy Focus

CHAPTER 1

Government and Policy: An Introduction

Governmental policy making is the response of government to stimuli coming from both the external and internal environments (that is, from events and conditions both outside and inside the government). In order to understand the nature and impact of the American national government as a policy actor—the aim of this volume—it must be viewed in the context of those environments.

A principal reason for the existence of any government, including the national government of the United States, stems from the nature of some of the general functions that must be performed in a society—functions that affect all or nearly all of the citizens in a given territorial area (what in modern terms is called the nation-state). These general matters seem best handled by a single general authority that we call a government. The most obvious general function that governments handle for society is defense; others include regulating commerce, maintaining domestic security and order, and providing for the welfare of citizens.

It is not inevitable that all governments will handle all of these functions (in feudal Europe, for example, even defense was not the sole prerogative of the central government) and there is, of course, nothing inevitable about the exact way in which those matters are handled, who makes decisions, what kinds of decisions are made, and who benefits and who does not benefit from the decisions. These elements vary a great deal from society to society and within a society through time. Choices about what the government does and does not handle, what is left for the private sector to handle, and how government authority is exercised are made over time in any given society and are usually in a state of at least slow change.

All government involves coercion. This does not mean that government is constantly forcing the citizenry to do something. Rather it means that the power to coerce is present and can, when necessary, be used. In a stable society most of the time coercion does not need to be used; the citizens simply obey a combination of formal laws and informal norms that help maintain whatever form of order is acceptable to the ruling authorities in that society. As one student of government has put it:

> Inevitably there is an element of coercion in collective life. Organization is a means of stabilizing relations among members of a collectivity so that, despite efforts of some to displace costs on the collective, a rough sharing of the costs of collective benefits can be made. Institutions are means of moralizing coercion. Administration is a means of routinizing coercion. Government is a means of legitimizing it. Power is simply the relative share a person or group appears to have in shaping and directing the instruments of coercion.[1]

In the United States the government is supposed to be representative of the citizens of the nation. The belief that the governed should have some say in how they are governed is widespread. Constraints on governmental policy emanate from

[1] Theodore J. Lowi, "Decision Making vs. Policy Making: Toward an Antidote for Technocracy." *Public Administration Review*, vol. 30 (May/June, 1970), p. 314.

the general population and from a variety of its specific parts. Yet the society is so large that there is no physical possibility of direct democracy—that is, continuous, detailed policy making by the whole citizenry—and so representative government is accepted as the most feasible alternative that will allow both a government that is able to work and one that takes into account the values, interests, and beliefs of the governed. As policies are adopted and implemented, the hope on the part of the governors is that they will be accepted as legitimate by all or at least most of the governed. If the institutions of government are viewed as legitimate by the population, then the policy decisions processed by those institutions are also likely to be accepted and obeyed, thus minimizing the likelihood that the elements of coercion (military or police power) will be actively used by the government.

In many ways, of course, separating the national government from other governments in the United States is artificial. All levels of government (as well as many private governments—corporations, banks, churches, unions, and so forth) make policy decisions that have considerable impact on the daily life of everyone. In some ways the national government is less visible to most people than either state and local governments or private governments, because the latter are usually responsible for administration of policies that directly affect the day-to-day lives of the citizens. Thus, if a citizen breaks an axle in a chuckhole, he blames the city. If a fifth-grade teacher has too many students, parents blame the local school board. If the price of bread goes up, customers blame the grocer or the bakery. If a state policeman is abusive, the aggrieved individual blames the state. Some of these experiences may even lead to the filing of complaints.

On the other hand, the national government may be indirectly involved in policies that are on the surface only local matters. For example, the city may not have resurfaced a bad road because aid expected from the Department of Transportation (perhaps administered through the State government) was not forthcoming. The overcrowded fifth-grade classroom may be the indirect result of a smaller congressional appropriation for the Elementary and Secondary Education Act than the

President and the Department of Health, Education, and Welfare had requested. The increased price of bread may have resulted from a threatened strike by the bakers union because of some action of the National Labor Relations Board. The patrolman's poor roadside manner may have been improved if funds for a training program on community relations sponsored by the Justice Department had been allocated by the federal Office of Management and Budget.

Of course, the national government is directly and immediately visible and important on at least a few occasions. Millions of American males know that Congress once passed something called the Selective Service Act that the President signed and that Congress and the President together provided a system for administering it. When people cut driving time in half on vacation trips across the country they became aware of an interstate highway system paid for by a mammoth trust fund created in 1956 by Congress and the President. If a black American has relatives entering integrated public schools for the first time, he no doubt is aware that the Supreme Court, lower federal courts, the Justice Department, and the Department of Health, Education, and Welfare have slowly acted out a policy drama that is resulting in desegregation.

The Meaning of Policy

The examples above suggest the wide range of policies in which the federal government is active. The study of governmental policy action without some organizing scheme for ordering observed phenomena would be at best random and difficult. To facilitate this task, a simplified framework for analyzing policy making in the federal government will be used in this text.[2]

As Figure 1–1 shows, the framework involves a set of inter-

[2] For a more detailed elaboration of this framework and an application to policy research, see Randall B. Ripley, William B. Moreland, and Richard H. Sinnreich, "Policy-Making: A Conceptual Scheme," *American Politics Quarterly*, vol. 1 (1973).

FIGURE 1-1. The Policy Arena

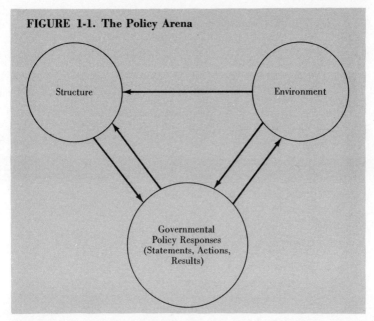

actions between three general concepts—structure, environment, and governmental policy responses—that together comprise the policy arena. Environmental characteristics can have a direct effect on both policy response and structure. Policy response can have a direct effect on both structure and environment.

The *governmental policy arena* is the locus of those governmental responses to the government's internal and external environments. These environments include statements of intent against which subsequent actions by the government and results in both government and society can be measured. In the language of psychology, policy making is the response of an organism called government to stimuli coming from the internal and external environments.

Structure contains characteristics, norms, and recurring patterns *inside* the government—for example, characteristics of agency maturity and agency personnel and decision-making patterns. *Environment*, by exclusion, denotes all those events,

7

conditions, and trends that are not part of the government—for example, election returns, public opinion, economic and social conditions and trends, and coalition behavior. *Policy response* denotes what the government does in responding to environment and structure. There are three elements to a policy response: statements, actions, and results.

A *policy statement* is a declaration of intent on the part of the government to do something. This declaration is sometimes highly visible—as in a statement by the President or in the passage by Congress of an important new statute. A policy statement can also be invisible to most of the public—as in a memo from a bureau chief to a subordinate. Not all statements by governmental actors are policy statements, however. The function of a policy statement is explicit in its attempt to order the responses of government. Accordingly, the policy statement always implies some choice among alternatives has been made.

Policy action is what the government actually does, as distinguished from what it says it is going to do (sometimes with many and conflicting voices) in its policy statement.

Just as not all statements can be considered policy statements, many actions cannot be considered policy actions. Often governmental actors behave in ways that have no bearing—positive or negative—on any previously expressed governmental intentions. Such behavior is essentially irrelevant to the policy arena, at least in the immediate sense However, the results of such actions may subsequently become important.

A *policy result* is what happens in society as a result of the government's policy statements and actions. A policy result is predicated upon the prior existence of both a policy statement *and* a policy action.

Several qualifications about this conception of policy should be entered at this point. First, although policy response is defined in terms of statements, actions, and results (that is, positive happenings), the government can choose, either consciously or unconsciously, not to act in a given field, and that choice also has consequences for the governed. Societal results may well stem in part from nonstatements and nonactions.

Thus, the agenda of the government is especially important. And just because some item is omitted from that agenda does not mean it is unimportant. For example, for many years neither poverty nor racial equality were on the federal agenda in any important and persistent way, but those problems were just as real before the federal government discovered them as they were after their discovery.

Second, not all public policy (that is, policy that has the potential of affecting a relatively large part of the public, at least because it is based on the use of resources that are collected from the public) is made by the government. The major economic institutions of the society that are formally outside government (for example, giant corporations or labor unions) also make policy statements and undertake policy actions that have widespread impact on large parts of the population and even have direct implications for the use of public resources. A major price decision by the automobile manufacturers will, for example, immediately affect potential new-car buyers. However, it may also have implications for how vigorously the government will pursue the imposition of antipollution standards on the engines used by the auto makers (antipollution devices are likely to add still more to the price of the car) or for how the government may view the continuance of an excise tax on cars (such a tax also raises the price; the repeal of such a tax would seemingly offset the price increase—a move that might be judged both economically justifiable and politically popular). In short, government is an important policy actor, but it is by no means the only actor involved in the production of public policy.

Basic Characteristics of the American National Government

The national government of the United States has many characteristics, but three are particularly striking: size, fragmentation, and incrementalism.

The national government is a huge enterprise with close to

9

three million civilian employees, another three million persons in the armed services, eleven major departments, more than forty independent agencies and regulatory commissions, a rather elaborate set of institutions collectively called the presidency, another elaborate set of institutions collectively called Congress and a large court system. All of these people and institutions are engaged in a large and varied number of policy areas.

The immensity of the government leads naturally to fragmentation—that is, many different parts that have, most of the time, only nominal ties with each other. This could also be called specialization, since different parts of the government specialize both in terms of subject matter and in terms of the chronological stage of policy activity.

Fragmentation (or specialization) means that in the American national government there is no single source of dynamism that can, in all issue areas on all occasions, be relied on to provide the impetus for some sort of activity. Likewise, there is no single element that can, in all issue areas on all occasions, be counted on to promote only inaction. Instead, the cues for both inaction and action may come from any of the various subunits of the government. Depending on what is at stake and the time period in question, the same subunit may on one occasion be a leading advocate of action and on another occasion a leading advocate of inaction. In some senses the President is the best placed official to give a series of cues for action; but even he is often on the side of inaction. And Congress, which is sometimes portrayed in the popular press as the roadblock to all action, is certainly capable of pushing dramatic action, as well as inaction.

Fragmentation is enhanced by the existence of many separate "subgovernments" that control most routine policy matters (and the overwhelming majority of all policy activity by the government is routine). These subgovernments are peopled by key officials from Congress, the bureaucracy, and the private sector (usually in the form of representatives of interest groups). Typically, a bureau chief and a few key subordinates, a subcommittee chairman and ranking minority member from each house of Congress, perhaps some of their key staff members, and a skilled lobbyist or two, all working together, will generate most of the action or inaction in some small segment of the total policy domain of the government.[3] And these subgovernments are usually isolated from one another. Less routine matters usually break out of these small subgovernments and a wider range of participants become involved.

American government proceeds incrementally on policy matters.[4] This means that changes in policy tend to come very slowly. Both the direction and the magnitude of change move by relatively small increments or decrements most of the time. This is not, however, either an inevitable or a universal situation. There are occasions when policy changes rapidly and dramatically, but most of the time change comes slowly and in small amounts.

The predominance of incremental change is a natural and unsurprising result of the government's size, complexity, and fragmentation. A large collection of issue-specific subgovernments in a complex government ordinarily operates through a series of bargains within and occasionally between those subgovernments. The bargains themselves are both implicit and explicit and conscious and unconscious. The nature of this bargaining, given always limited resources, helps lead to gradual growth or shrinkage in most areas of policy at any given time.

Symbolically, nine times out of ten in any period of time a change in a policy or program x will be $x + 1$ or $x - 1$ rather than $x + 10$ or $x - 10$ when compared to the immediately

[3] J. Leiper Freeman, *The Political Process* (New York: Random House, 1967). Ernest S. Griffith, *Congress: Its Contemporary Role*, 3rd ed. (New York: New York University Press, 1961). The term "subgovernments" comes from Douglass Cater, *Power in Washington* (New York: Random House, 1964).

[4] Charles E. Lindblom, *The Intelligence of Democracy* (New York: The Free Press, 1965). Randall B. Ripley, "Interagency Committees and Incrementalism: the Case of Aid to India," *Midwest Journal of Political Science*, vol. 8 (May, 1964), pp. 143–165. Ira Sharkansky, *The Routines of Politics* (New York: Van Nostrand Reinhold Company, 1970). Aaron Wildavsky, *The Politics of the Budgetary Process* (Boston: Little, Brown and Company, 1964).

preceding time period. Only in the one case out of ten will the $x + 10$ or the $x - 10$ situation occur.

The Growth of Policy Activity by the American National Government

The history of the American national government has, in general, been a history of expanding policy activity. In world affairs the United States has, in this century, taken an increasing activist stance. In the domestic sphere, three general kinds of governmental activity have evolved at different times—subsidy, regulation, and manipulation.[5]

From the beginning of the nation until the Civil War the broadest goal of the federal government was to expand the field of economic opportunity for all white Americans by selective governmental actions. Thus, the controversies over the Louisiana Purchase, Texas, Oregon, "manifest destiny," internal improvements, railroad building, homesteads, and the tariffs were all posing the same choice: should the government help expand the opportunity for individual (and, increasingly, corporate) Americans to succeed economically by offering some kind of subsidy, or should the government do nothing? The country almost always opted in favor of the subsidizing activity. Subsidy thus came to be accepted as a legitimate endeavor for the central government to undertake.

Following the Civil War new problems began to arise that involved public discussion of what the government should do. Corporate wealth, which rapidly made the Republican Party its political handmaiden, began to alter the dimensions of American opportunity. The end of the homesteading era and the massive waves of immigration from eastern and southern Europe presented new kinds of problems.

The political system took about twenty years to frame even the beginnings of a coherent response. The response came in

[5] This section is adapted from the introduction to my reader, *Public Policies and their Politics* (New York: Norton, 1966).

the form of adding regulation to the legitimate sphere of governmental activity. Thus slowly, unsurely, and hesitatingly the government began to tell the owners of railroads and the formers of trusts that they could not behave in certain ways. Members of the Republican party formerly subservient to business interests were willing to deliver this message to their erstwhile friends. In the late nineteenth century Congress began the long development of railroad regulation and anti-trust activity with passage of the Interstate Commerce Act in 1887 and the Sherman Antitrust Act in 1890. In the first fifteen years of the twentieth century new laws pursued the same ends. Several laws in the first decade of the new century tightened railroad regulation. The first two years of Woodrow Wilson's presidency (1913 and 1914) saw the passage of the Clayton Act and the Federal Trade Commission Act, both aimed at the trusts and at restraint of trade in general. Related major laws such as the Underwood-Simmons Tariff and the Federal Reserve Act were also designed to make American business pursue profit honestly.

It took the catastrophe of an economic depression, seemingly irreversible by normal means, to introduce and legitimize the third line of activity—manipulation on the part of the federal government. The economic disaster of the 1930s revealed the corresponding social disaster that had been developing for a number of decades. The government was given authority to relieve both economic and social deprivation and to prevent the recurrence of at least the most visible parts of both of them. Now the government could, with the approval of a majority of the nation's citizens, attempt to change the environment of those citizens so that the gulf between the indulged and deprived might shrink.

It took yet another crisis—the involvement of the nation in World War II—to expand even further the sphere of manipulative government action. The government was given responsibility for control of prices, wages, rents, and profits. Eventually, the social upheavals caused by the war made race the province of substantial government activity.

Thus, by the 1970s governmental techniques of influencing

what goes on in the private sphere and, in a sense, of mingling the public and private orders, could legitimately be aimed at three things: the rate of private activity (where techniques of subsidy could be used), the conditions under which private activity could take place (where techniques of regulation could be used), and the rewards for private activity (where techniques of manipulation could be used). Controversy still erupts over specific uses of the techniques, but government activities using these classes of techniques are widely accepted as legitimate.

PART 2

The Environment for Government Activity

CHAPTER 2

Public Opinion

This chapter opens a section dealing with the concept of linkage between the government and the public over which the government rules. This concept is interesting from a practical point of view—from the point of view of a citizen pondering whether and how he can influence the government. It is also interesting from an analytical point of view—from the point of view of a political scientist asking where influence is exerted by whom, what channels allow access of the citizen to the government, and what kind of behavior is characteristic of citizens and government officials as influence is sought and gained in some cases and denied in others.

There are several widely varying views about the interplay between government and public and about the effect that public opinion has on the government's policy responses. One argument, grounded in democratic ideals, proposes that the public has a direct role in the making of policy because it knows the policy positions of candidates and it elects officials on the basis of policy positions—officials whom, once elected, pay attention to the preferences of the public. A more elitist position states that the public is poorly qualified to advise government officials because it is not educated in most policy areas and it is unaware of the policy positions of the candidates. This position argues that officials can and should make policy without much regard for public opinion. A third position, falling between these two, maintains that while in a representative government officials cannot afford to be habitually insensitive to the opinions of the public, public opinion is not the only factor to which officials respond as they shape policy.

The view presented in this text coincides most closely with the third position: In general, public opinion sets the bounds within which officials can act. It by no means dictates all policy responses, but on the other hand it is not simply molded by officials. As the place of public opinion in policy making is examined in this chapter, several areas will be discussed: the characteristics of opinion, the influence of family and groups on opinion, the impact of political leaders on opinion, the impact of the mass media on opinion, and the impact of public opinion on governmental policy response.

What Does Public Opinion Mean?

What is public opinion? What does it look like and how is it defined? First of all, opinion is not a single, unified, static entity. There is no one thing walking around in the real world that we can point to and say, "That is public opinion," although in writing and speaking, we often tend to personify public opinion and treat it as if it were a real entity.

Opinion is a potentially confusing concept, because it occurs in many shapes and varieties and comes from many different sources. For example, we speak of an individual's personal opinions and his political opinions; we speak of elite opinion, mass opinion, special publics, the mass public, and so on. All of these topics deserve attention, but for present purposes this discussion will focus on the opinion of the individual—what its characteristics are, how it is formed in early life, and what forces act on an opinion to change it in later life.

A lone opinion obviously does not constitute public opinion; public opinion is the expressed set of views held by a large number of people on some issue of general importance.[1] Mass opinion is the opinion that is attributed to the general or mass public (the adult population). Knowledge of this opinion is procured by aggregating the results of systematic sampling and interviewing of individuals. Elite or special opinion is the opinion representative of a particular group, either formal or informal.

Obviously not all peoeple are going to hold the same view on an issue. Some may feel affirmatively; some may feel negatively; and some may have no opinion at all. Some may feel very strongly; others may care only a little or not at all. Officials in all branches of government also hold a variety of views with varying degrees of intensity. Items get added to the agenda of government when portions of the public and officials who hold the same views intensely come in contact with each other and initiate a series of interactions that can eventually lead to governmental policy statements and actions.

Among the attributes of opinion are the *subject* (opinion is focused on something), the *directional content* (there is either a positive or negative affect toward the subject), the *intensity* (the opinion is held with some degree of strength or weakness), and the *stability* (over time, the direction and intensity of an opinion will either remain the same, or they will change with varying degrees of difficulty).

To illustrate the different kinds of atttributes of opinion, let us assume that four different individuals have the following opinions on the subject of gun-control legislation in two different years:

Smith in 1968: "Gun control is absolutely essential. The murders of Bobby Kennedy and Martin Luther King would not have happened if we had controlled the purchase of guns."

---

[1] Bernard C. Hennessey, *Public Opinion*, 2nd ed. (Belmont, Calif.: Wadsworth, 1971), p. 30.

Smith in 1974: "We have to control guns. I don't agree with George Wallace, but this shooting in 1972 is just another example of what happens when guns can be purchased by any nut."

Jones in 1968: "I guess I am for gun control. There's a lot of crime and killing, and gun control might help reduce that."

Jones in 1974: "I doubt if gun control would do much good. What we need is more police."

Brown in 1968: "I am against gun-control legislation. It would just create another bureaucracy. The goal of keeping guns out of the hands of criminals is a good one, but I doubt that gun-control legislation would reach that goal."

Brown in 1974: "We might as well try gun-control legislation. Nothing else seems to work, and we have to find some way to cut down on violence and crime."

Green in 1968: "It is absolutely unconstitutional to have gun-control legislation. Americans have always prided themselves in being able to maintain arms. The communists or somebody like that must be promoting this gun-control business, and they are using the Kennedy and King assassinations to whip up hysteria."

Green in 1974: "Gun control is screwy. It would deny a man the right to enjoy his leisure time by hunting. It also goes against the constitutional guarantee of the right to bear arms."

Obviously the subject of these opinions is gun-control legislation. The direction of opinion is favorable to such legislation in the cases of Smith in both years, Jones in 1968, and Brown in 1974. The direction is against such legislation in the cases of Green in both years, Jones in 1974, and Brown in 1968. The intensity of opinion is high in the cases of Smith and Green in both years. It is low in the cases of Jones and Brown in both years. The stability of opinion is high in the cases of Smith and Green in both years (they both felt the same way in both years and had a high degree of intensity in both years). Stability is low in the cases of Jones and Brown (they both changed their minds, although neither of them felt very intensely in either year).

Persons may hold more than one opinion on a given subject. Such related opinions are called *opinion clusters;* they share the attributes listed above, as well as additional qualities. Lane and Sears include among the characteristics of opinion clusters [2]: informational content (the degree of differentiation and the awareness of the implications of an opinion), organization (the degree of conscious integration of opinions, their breadth, and the frame of reference within which opinions are held), consistency (the degree of internal consistency between constituent opinions in an opinion cluster), the policy component (the difference between stated opinions and observed actions), and salience (those clusters or opinions within a cluster that are most important for organizing one's thoughts and behavior).

Any topic is potentially capable of evoking opinion from a diverse number of publics, ranging from the individual all the way through formal and informal groups to the mass public. The divisions between these publics are not formal or rigid barriers—there is a great deal of movement all along the spectrum. Any citizen may simultaneously hold opinions as an individual, a member of the National Farmers Organization, a member of the special public interested in promoting employment opportunities for veterans, and a member of the mass public.

Some publics are more likely to hold and express opinions than others. In general, on most issues the mass public is least likely to become interested, informed, and opinionated. On most matters, mass-public opinion is characterized by low-intensity and low-ideological coherence. There are some issues that can mobilize mass opinion, such as war, depression, and major social change; but most issues go unnoticed by large numbers of people.

What Key has called attentive publics [3] and what is here referred to as specialized or elite publics are interested informal groups that form around a particular issue or set of issues.

[2] Robert E. Lane and David O. Sears, *Public Opinion* (Englewood Cliffs, N.J.: Prentice-Hall, 1964), pp. 11–15.

[3] V. O. Key, Jr., *Public Opinion and American Democracy* (New York: Knopf, 1961), p. 544.

While for any issue there is likely to be at least one specialized public holding opinion(s), it is not likely that the same attentive public will be present on a wide range of issues. As conceived of here, the specialized public is a transient group, bound together only by common interest in an issue.

Issues that have been accepted and are viewed as more or less permanently settled (for example, an issue on which mass-public opinion has exhibited a stable, persistent unanimity of direction) do not usually evoke expressed opinion unless some event challenges what has been accepted.

To take an extreme example, it is probably settled in the United States that at least two major parties can legitimately compete for public offices without hindrance or harassment. If the party in power were to institute a program of systematic execution of the leaders of the major party out of power, such action would undoubtedly mobilize negative expressions of opinion. Unless such action were taken, however, few people would think to express an opinion on the issue. Public-opinion polls do not ask questions like, "Do you favor the execution of Democratic party (or Republican party) leaders?" Nor are individuals likely to put such a question to themselves when they think about political matters.

On other issues, however—those that are not settled—the normal situation is for different groups to hold different opinions.

Stability of opinion varies from issue area to issue area. Three ideal patterns typify what occurs. The first pattern is one of stability over time. An example is the attitude of the American public, in the period between 1953 and 1964, toward free speech for communists. Table 2–1 summarizes the response to the question, "Do you think members of the Communist party in this country should be allowed to speak on the radio?" The division of opinion on this issue was virtually unchanged from 1953 to 1964.

The second pattern is one of instability and unpredictability. If opinion is sampled over a long period of time, a cyclical pattern might emerge. Or it is possible that the subject area is one that produces aberrant periods in what is otherwise a rela-

TABLE 2-1. Public Opinion and Freedom of Speech, 1953-64

Year of Poll	For Complete Freedom of Speech	Oppose or Want Limited	No Opinion
1953	19%	77%	4%
1957	17%	80%	3%
1964	18%	77%	5%

Source: Compiled from data in the *Public Opinion Quarterly*, vol. 34 (fall, 1970), p. 488.

tively stable opinion. Or there may be no predictable pattern at all. An example of this pattern of instability is provided by American attitudes toward capital punishment. Table 2–2 represents unstable opinion (in response to the question, "Are you in favor of the death penalty for persons convicted of murder?") The fluctuations of opinion on this issue follow no identifiable patttern.

The third pattern is one of change in a consistent direction. A good example is the opinion of Americans on the seating of Communist China in the United Nations, which is summarized in Table 2–3. The proportion of Americans favoring the seat-

TABLE 2-2. Public Opinion and Capital Punishment, 1936-69

Year of Poll	For Capital Punishment	Against	No Opinion
1936[a]	62%	33%	5%
1953	68%	25%	7%
1960	51%	36%	13%
1965	45%	43%	12%
1966	42%	47%	11%
1969	51%	40%	9%

Source: Compiled from data in the *Public Opinion Quarterly*, vol. 34 (summer, 1970), p. 291.

a. The 1936 question was worded slightly differently from that given in the text: "Are you in favor of the death penalty for murder?"

TABLE 2-3. Public Opinion toward Admitting Communist China to the U.N., 1954-70

Year of Poll	Favor	Oppose	No Opinion
1954	7%	78%	15%
1957	13%	70%	17%
1961	20%	64%	16%
1965	22%	64%	14%
1970	35%	49%	16%
1971	45%	38%	17%

Source: *Public Opinion Quarterly*, vol. 35 (spring, 1971), p. 125. *Gallup Opinion Index*, report no. 72 (June, 1971), p. 16.

ing of the People's Republic grew steadily from 1954 to 1971.

The intensity of mass opinion can vary, but generally intensity is low on most issues. Only rarely does an issue stimulate intense opinion on the part of the American mass public. At any period of time, of course, there are almost always special publics that feel intensely about a variety of specific issues.

Public opinion also tends to be marked by ideological inconsistency. That is, people often hold opinions that are not ideologically consistent with each other—or at least so it appears to analysts. For example, in 1968 Senator Eugene McCarthy ran against President Lyndon Johnson in the New Hampshire primary election on the basis of his opposition to the war in Vietnam. Studies have shown that those who supported McCarthy were, on the average, more in favor of the war than those who supported Johnson.[4] Here the inconsistency came between opinions about men (McCarthy and Johnson) and opinions about the war. Many who voted in New Hampshire did not make the link that McCarthy himself saw and proclaimed and that analysts accepted.

Another kind of inconsistency of opinion involves the inability to make the link between a general opinion and a specific

[4] Richard M. Scammon and Ben J. Wattenberg, *The Real Majority*, 2nd ed. (New York: Coward, McCann, 1970), p. 91.

application of that opinion. For example, in 1940, ninety-seven percent of a national sample said they believed in freedom of speech, but seventy-six percent of that same sample said they wanted at least some restrictions on allowing communists and fascists to hold meetings and express their views in this country.[5]

The most normal inconsistency is one in which large bodies of public opinion do not break the same way on a variety of highly visible and important issues. Table 2–4 illustrates three of many possible patterns. This table portrays the opinions of three hypothetical samples of people (not necessarily organized groups) on four different issues. Case A represents ideological consistency of opinions—the group takes what might be portrayed as consistently "liberal" positions on each issue.

In Case B the sample's opinions represent ideological specialization—there is only one issue about which it holds an opinion. For a variety of reasons this group holds no opinion (is apathetic) on the other issues.

Case C describes a situation in which internal inconsistencies exist within the opinion set. Thus, Group C is for the expansion of the government's role in the promotion of full employment and for restricting the role of the military, but it is against government efforts to expand racial justice, and it opposes attempts to limit governmental invasion of privacy. This kind of inconsistency is not unusual, especially for the mass public. Inconsistency depends on how salient and important particular issues are to the individual and how intensely he or she feels about them. Also, it should be noted that inconsistency does not imply irrationality. Group C may be perfectly rational in its choices, but to an outside observer, ideological consistency seems to be missing.

Most of the time the opinion of any group of American citizens, large or small, formal or informal, will look like Case B or C; only rarely does it look like Case A.

[5] *Public Opinion Quarterly*, vol. 34 (fall, 1970), p. 486.

TABLE 2-4. Examples of Ideological Consistency and Inconsistency

ISSUE:	Restrict the Role of the Military in American Life	Expand Government Efforts to Increase Racial Justice	Increase Government Efforts to Decrease Unemployment	Limit Government Invasion of Privacy
Case A — Ideological Consistency	+	+	+	+
Case B — Ideological Specialization	0	+	0	0
Case C — Ideological Inconsistency	+	−	+	−

Key: + = Favors
− = Opposes
0 = Holds no opinion

The Influence of Family on Political Opinions

Social psychology evidence strongly suggests that opinions, including political opinions, are held by an individual before he seeks information and rationales for those opinions. In most cases, information seeking and reasoning are engaged in to support an opinion already held.

One of the earliest political topics on which a child forms an opinion is party identification.[6] The influence of the family in shaping the child's basic party identification is greater than any other influence on party identification. It is also the most important political impact that the family has. Table 2–5 summarizes some data on children's political preference. As the table shows, when both parents hold the same party identification, the child is much more likely to identify with that party; when parents do not have the same party identification, the children tend to be independents.

Hess and Torney found that many children consciously called themselves independents rather than Republicans or Democrats. This may be a partial result of the way in which schools socialize political attitudes—teachers tend not to emphasize partisanship and divisiveness but to stress the ideals of independence, civic duty, and candidate evaluation.[7]

A balanced conclusion regarding the effectiveness of the family in transmitting political attitudes is reported by Hess and Torney:

> The effectiveness of the family in transmitting attitudes has been overestimated in previous research. The family transmits preference for a political party, but in most other areas its most effective role is to support other institutions in teaching political information and orientations. . . . Aside from party preference, the influence of the family seems to be primarily indirect and to influence attitudes toward authority, rules, and compliance.[8]

[6] Robert D. Hess and Judith V. Torney, *The Development of Political Attitudes in Children* (Garden City, N.Y.: Doubleday, 1968).

[7] *Ibid.*, p. 248.

[8] *Ibid.*, p. 247.

TABLE 2-5. Parental Influence and Party Preference, 1968

Respondent's Party Preference	Parents' Party Identification			
	Both Parents Democrat	Both Parents Republican	Parents Inconsistent	Other
Democrat	69%	21%	30%	45%
Republican	7%	58%	24%	19%
Independent	21%	19%	43%	28%
Other	3%	2%	4%	8%
Total (N = 1673)	100% (705)	100% (336)	101%[a] (230)	100% (402)

Source: Compiled from Survey Research Center (University of Michigan) data.

[a]Does not total to 100 because of rounding.

Formation of opinion on ideological (that is, liberal-conservative) issues also begins in childhood and is fairly advanced and stable by the end of high school.[9] Again the family is an important agent for shaping the child's ideological orientations, but there is also interplay between the child and other influences, particularly his perception of social and economic class.

An individual's political opinions, including party identification, are subjected to many potentially disruptive forces after he leaves the family's close orbit of influence. Below, we shall discuss the durability of the political attitudes imparted by the family as a socializing force.[10]

In general, the rebellion of an adolescent against parental standards, authority, and values does not have political effect. The youth may reject his parents' middle-class grooming habits and moral standards, but he is likely to retain the basic party identification imparted to him by the family. When a youth does reject his party identification, he may well reject the whole political system as well, at least temporarily.

Increasing education does not seem to work in favor of one party or the other. More Republican parents can afford college for their children than Democratic parents and so more Republican-leaning students enter college than do those who lean Democratic. And, in general, both groups emerge with the same leanings with which they began. The exception to this generalization is that the proportion of college students identifying themselves as independents has gone up sharply in recent years, at the expense of both parties.

Higher education also has a mixed impact on political opinions (as differentiated from party identification). Such education is positively associated with more tolerant attitudes toward nonconformity.[11]

The impact of higher education on opinion about the Viet-

[9] Robert E. Lane and David O. Sears, *op. cit.*, p. 22.

[10] This discussion is based on *ibid.*, pp. 23–29.

[11] Samuel A. Stouffer, *Communism, Conformity, and Civil Liberties* (Garden City, N.Y.: Doubleday, 1955), p. 90.

nam War is complex.[12] In general, individuals who had at least some higher education in small colleges and in less prestigious institutions were more "hawkish" than the general population. Individuals who had attended elite schools were more "dovish" than the general population. Given that the number of individuals attending schools in the elite category is a very small proportion of all individuals with some college education, it turns out that, in general, the impact of education seems to have been in the direction of "hawkishness" on Vietnam.

Social mobility produces most of the political movement away from the party preferences of the family. This is particularly true of young adults in their 20s. Typically, individuals in their 20s are both socially and geographically mobile. If an individual is to begin a career that will place him in a substantially different socio-economic status or class than his parents, he usually will begin that career in his 20s. Young families of this age are also likely to move several times before they settle on their final city and neighborhood within that city. By the age of 30, most young adults have set their sights on what is feasible in terms of career aspirations and in terms of class or social mobility. Most have children by age 30 and may have at least a rough idea of their ultimate family size, and that also provides a stabilizing factor. Also, people in their 30s tend to have chosen their social set, and this set holds views that are highly reinforcing of the views of any individual in the set. For example, political agreement among close friends increases with age. This is illustrated in Table 2–6.

What happens to the political beliefs and party identification of people who do perceive themselves to be moving upward or downward in society? Young adults who think of themselves as moving upward tend to adopt the political party identification (usually Republican) of the new, higher class to which they aspire. At the same time they will often retain the ideology of their parents and former class (often a more liberal or Democratic ideology). Those who perceive themselves to be moving downward from middle-class status tend to retain

[12] Philip E. Converse and Howard Schuman, "'Silent Majorities' and the Vietnam War," *Scientific American*, vol. 222 (June, 1970), pp. 17–25.

TABLE 2-6. Age and Political Agreement

Age	Percent of Three Best Friends Who Vote the Same as the Respondent
21-25	53%
26-34	69%
35-44	75%
Over 45	77%

Source: Bernard R. Berelson, Paul F. Lazarsfeld, and William N. McPhee, *Voting* (Chicago: University of Chicago Press, 1954), p. 97.

their party identification (often Republican) but accept much of the ideology of the working class favoring social-welfare measures. Thus, both upward and downward mobility create a disjunction between ideology and party identification. In both cases the Republican party tends to gain but a more liberal ideology also tends to gain. This may help explain why Republican leaders gradually and grudgingly accept some moderately liberal positions on domestic issues. It may also help explain Republican presidential victories despite an electorate that is, in terms of professed self-identification, Democratic. It is also interesting to note that those who experience or perceive mobility generally do not abandon the whole of the parental political tradition—usually they retain either the party or the political beliefs of their parents.[13]

The Influence of Groups on Political Opinions

Groups other than families also have potent influence on the party and ideological views of the individual. These groups include clusters of co-workers, unions, lodges, business groups, farm groups, and church congregations. Some of the groups

[13] Robert E. Lane and David O. Sears, *op. cit.,* p. 129.

involve a great deal of face-to-face contact; others are a good deal more impersonal.

Every individual belongs to at least a few groups, and everyone has experienced pressure to conform to group norms and opinions in varying degrees. The impact of groups on an individual's opinions may be either to reinforce or to erode the views he inherited from family socialization, depending on whether the individual belongs to groups whose views deviate from those he learned from the family.

Many different factors related to issue, setting, and individual and group characteristics influence the effectiveness of the group in producing conformity among members. Lane and Sears have summarized the findings of social science research in this area.[14] A number of group characteristics can increase the pressure to conform:

1. Small size of the group.
2. High interaction, especially over a long period of time, among members of the group.
3. High agreement among most members of the group on a specific issue.
4. High degree of cohesiveness in the group in general.
5. High relevance of a given issue to the purposes of the group.
6. High perception of threat to group goals.
7. High need on the part of individuals for the services provided by the group.

Group norms need not always be in operation to produce conformity. People often shape their attitudes and opinions in response to perceived pressures from the group, even when these pressures are not operating.[15]

Individuals often belong to groups that put cross-pressures on them. A person who is a member of a liberal union (for example, the United Auto Workers) and a fundamentalist Protestant church may well be exposed to radically differing

[14] *Ibid.*, pp. 35–36.
[15] Ivan D. Steiner, "Primary Group Influences on Public Opinion," *American Sociological Review*, vol. 19 (1954), p. 267.

opinions on the place of blacks in society. A person who is a member of the management group of a corporation dependent on an extractive industry for its economic welfare (for example, strip mining) and who also belongs to the Sierra Club or other similar environmentalist groups will almost surely feel cross-pressures.

Persons in such positions usually seek some rationalization that will allow them to maintain both memberships while diminishing anxiety induced by the differing stands of the groups. They may, for example, decide the issue in conflict is not important. Or they may decide that the issue is not really vital to one of the groups, and therefore they are justified in adopting the opinion of the other. If the conflict becomes intense they may well drop out of active participation in one group. If it becomes unbearable they may simply sever ties with one group.

The Influence of Leaders on Mass-Public Opinion

Political leaders help shape opinion; they are not merely swayed by it. However, the best evidence from social science research indicates that the mass is not easily manipulated by political leaders. Susceptibility to attempts at manipulating mass opinion increases when the social scene is in a state of change (for example, dramatically shifting economic conditions) or when there is widely perceived threat (such as a war). In such situations, many familiar reference points disappear or shift, and people are more likely to take the leaders' cue.

Each "normal" situation in which leaders may influence opinion can be handled by individuals in a variety of ways, most of which allow the individual to minimize the change in his own opinion. Individuals have a number of psychological processes that allow them to hear what they want to hear (reinforcing statements) and to ignore what they do not want to hear (conflicting statements).

In a situation in which a leader is attempting to bring about a change in an individual's opinion and the individual is faced with conflict or dissonance among his own opinions, his opinion of the source, and his perception of the source's position, he will react in a way to relieve the dissonance. Exactly what his reaction will be depends on the relative strength of the three elements just named; in general he will change whichever element is easiest for him to change and that causes least change in his cognitive structure. Of course, the change desired by the leader would be change in the opinion held by the individual, but this is likely to occur only if the issue is one that is viewed as relatively unimportant by the individual or if it is not an intensely held opinion or both. As importance of the issue and intensity of the opinion increase, the likelihood of opinion change decreases.

There are other ways besides changing the opinion on the issue to respond to an influence situation that produces dissonance.[16] The individual can negatively reevaluate the source of influence; by decreasing its importance in his own mind, he need no longer regard the source as seriously as he would have previously. He can distort the source's position on an issue by seeing things in the message that were not intended but that are pleasing to the receiver. He can simply disbelieve what he hears from a particular source—by attributing it to a misquotation in a newspaper, for example. He can reorganize an entire set of beliefs so that the new position being urged upon him no longer offends. Obviously, this last alternative requires the most effort, and it would be likely to occur only rarely.

An example may be useful in illustrating the alternative responses mentioned above. Individual A believes in strong penalties for the possession and use of marijuana. Individual A respects Congressman X (and voted for him in the last election). Congressman X has issued a widely publicized statement concerning drastically reducing the penalties for first offenders under the present possession and use laws. A's possible reactions could be:

---

[16] Robert E. Lane and David O. Sears, *op. cit.*, pp. 47–52, offers a fuller discussion of these modes of managing conflict.

1. He may modify his own opinion to accommodate the statement made by X. This is likely if his opinion is not strongly held, if he does not feel the issue is very important, or if his opinion of and respect for X override his feelings on the issue.

2. He may lower his opinion of Congressman X and decide not to vote for him in the next election. This alternative is likely if his opinion is intense or if he views the issue as very important.

3. He may distort the statement made by X to accommodate his own views. For example, he may say, "X obviously intended only to raise the issue for review and debate by Congress—with the possibility that penalties be made weaker or stiffer or remain unchanged." This is likely if his opinion on the issue is intense, if he views the issue an important one, and if his opinion of Congressman X is also very high.

4. He may simply refuse to believe what has been attributed to X, blaming a misprint or a misquotation. This is likely if the opinion is intense, if the issue is viewed as important, and if the source is highly regarded.

5. He may juggle the opinion cluster (of which his feelings on marijuana penalties are a part) in order to rationalize the discrepancy by concentrating on the opinions of Congressman X on related issues that are aligned with his own views and by de-emphasizing the importance of the dissonant opinion. For example, he could say, "Congressman X favors much stronger enforcement of laws against 'hard' narcotics, and therefore his position on penalties for marijuana really isn't very important."

In short, the effectiveness of leaders in shaping mass opinion depends very much on a two-way interaction between the audience of the leaders and the leaders. Leaders can and do wield influence, but their effectiveness depends much on the receptivity of the audience, as well as on the environmental setting. In periods of great crisis or social upheaval, people are more susceptible to leaders' efforts to shape opinion.

The Impact of Mass Media on Public Opinion

The mass media have an impact on public opinion but cannot control it absolutely. Specific generalizations about the impact of the mass media on public opinion that have been supported through empirical research follow.[17]

Mass media are much more likely to reinforce existing opinions of those exposed to the media both directly and indirectly than they are likely to effect major changes in those opinions. The impact of the media is likely to be greatest on people who have not previously held an opinion on the subject in question. This means that "new" issues in politics afford the media the most chance for impact. For example, the media seem to have a greater impact on opinions about foreign affairs than about domestic affairs. Minor changes in existing opinions can be effected by the media. Also there seems to be evidence that repeated themes in the media can affect the intensity and direction of mass-public opinion.

Occasionally, the media convey a message that is potent in producing a change of opinion (conversion) on the part of large numbers of people. The possibility of this happening is probably increased in unstable social situations. In addition to the occasional changing of specific opinions, the media, particularly television, can also "undermine or bolster public confidence in the viability of political institutions and in the ability of political leaders to discharge their responsibilities." [18]

The media may have an indirect impact on mass opinion through having an impact on the opinion of elites or leaders and officials. Some leaders and officials, for example, may adopt a different style of behavior so as to look good on television. Specific elites may pay particular attention to certain publications or television commentators and be highly influenced by them and thus pass on those influences to other parts of the public as they seek to influence them.

---

[17] Joseph T. Klapper, *The Effects of Mass Communication* (New York: The Free Press, 1960). V. O. Key, Jr., *op. cit.*, pp. 400–409. Kurt Lang and Gladys E. Lang, *Politics and Television* (Chicago: Quadrangle, 1968).

[18] Kurt Lang and Gladys E. Lang, *op. cit.*, p. 306.

The Impact of Opinion on Governmental Policy Responses and on the Existence and Functioning of the Government

THE MULTITUDE OF PUBLICS

As indicated at the beginning of this chapter, there are a multitude of "publics" that have varying degrees of impact on the shaping of governmental policy responses. In addition to the mass public, there are also numerous, smaller publics that can be classed according to issue and function. The number of these specialized publics is limited only by the number of issue areas about which groups may form. These specialized publics may be either unorganized or may be formed into more permanent organized interest groups. A third kind of specialized public is made up by the members of the federal bureaucracy who are responsible for administering policy. A fourth kind is formed by state and local party leaders and government officials.

The opinions of all of these publics are involved in affecting governmental policy responses. The public that is most consistently involved, however, regardless of issue area, is the federal bureaucracy, since policy administration is an integral component of policy response, and since it is the rederal bureaucracy that is responsible for administering the policies of the federal government. In addition, many issues fail to stimulate interest at other levels of opinion, and even among interested publics there often may be divided opinion. A pattern of considerable apathy and some division of opinion gives a good deal of leeway to governmental officials, both elected and appointed, in inserting and acting on their own preferences.

THE ROLE OF MASS OPINION

Mass-public opinion does not control the shaping of specific governmental policy responses in the United States. But mass-public opinion does play an important part in allowing the government to exist and function in the policy arena at all.[19]

[19] The discussion in this section is elaborated more fully in John C. Wahlke, "Policy Demands and System Support: The Role of the Represented," *British Journal of Political Science*, vol. 1 (July, 1971), pp. 271–290.

There are those who argue that citizens should make specific policy demands both as individuals and as members of various kinds of groups and that the government should respond in detail to those demands. Constituency influence and group pressure convey the message from the citizenry to the government. Elections are both specific policy mandates for the future and render judgments about the policy performance of the past.

This position has considerable appeal as a statement of what government-citizen linkage *ought* to look like. However, as a statement of what *is*, it conflicts with a number of observations about the political behavior of the American citizenry and electorate. For example, empirical research has shown that few citizens have clearly developed policy preferences at the specific level, and most lack the instrumental knowledge about the structure and functioning of their political system that would enable them to communicate a policy preference if they held one. Most citizens never communicate with their representatives at all, and citizen knowledge of the policy-making activities and policy stances of their representatives is limited.

This situation does not mean impotence for the mass public, however. It still plays a critical role in allowing the government to exist and function at all. Specific support (or withholding of support) for specific policies may not often occur, but diffuse support for "the system" and some specific parts of it is necessary for its functioning. John Wahlke [20] has argued persuasively that public support for political community, political regime, and political authorities is essential for stability in the political system.[21]

If a political community is to continue its existence, then a

[20] *Ibid.*

[21] *Political community* refers to the willingness and ability of a group of people to work together to deal with political matters. *Political regime* refers to the norms and values that structure the way political decisions are made over time, that is, the rules of the game. *Political authorities* are simply those persons who hold positions of political leadership. For fuller elaboration of these concepts, see David Easton, *A Systems Analysis for Political Life* (New York: Wiley, 1965).

very large proportion of the population must have feelings of national loyalty. If sizable separatist segments emerge, political community is likely to become impossible. Northern Ireland, for example, may not be a viable political community.

Support for the political regime consists of a high level of acceptance of the rules of the game by which politics is played and of specific institutional arrangements in existence and a widespread willlingness on the part of a large majority of the population to comply with specific policy decisions, regardless of their content and regardless of their agreement or disagreement with them.

Support for political authorities is expressed or withheld through the electoral process.

The level of support necessary for the maintenance of political community and political regime has not been established empirically. In a system of free elections, of course, political authorities are supported by electoral pluralities, and while the withholding of support (as in the defeat of incumbent office holders) may be traumatic for the individuals involved, it is not traumatic for the system. If sizable minorities withheld support for the regime or even for the political community, however, the entire system could be changed dramatically.

Little systematic and thorough empirical research has been addressed to the question of the varying degrees of support present in the United States for political community and political regime (a great deal of systematic inquiry has been expended on elections and the support for political authorities), but some provocative findings have been produced on a scattered basis. For example, one set of findings on the public's view of politics and politicians suggest a deep reserve of respect.[22] When asked how they would feel if their son became a United States senator or representative, less than five percent of a national sample said they would have any reservations. The overwhelming majority said they would feel enormously proud. When asked to describe their general idea of a United States

[22] See the testimony of Franklin P. Kilpatrick before the House Committee on Standards of Official Conduct, Ninetieth Congress, first session (August 16, 1967), pp. 18–19.

congressman, favorable replies outweighed unfavorable replies by nine to one. This respect, however, does not necessarily generate confidence in the institutions in which these individuals serve. Such confidence has, in recent years, been declining.

On the other hand, recent studies indicate that race may be an important variable affecting one's outlook of the political system. Blacks have not completely given up on the established

TABLE 2-7. Views of Effectiveness of Government in Solving Urban Problems, by Race and Level of Government

	Black	White
Trying as Hard as They Can		
City Government	47%	65%
State Government	33%	41%
Federal Government	39%	51%
Trying Fairly Hard		
City Government	19%	16%
State Government	22%	23%
Federal Government	25%	21%
Trying Not Hard at All		
City Government	24%	13%
State Government	32%	25%
Federal Government	25%	21%

Source: *Kerner Commission Report, Supplemental Studies*, p. 45.

The questions used: "Do you think the Mayor of (Central City) is trying as hard as he can to solve the main problems of the city or that he is not doing all he could to solve these problems?" (If not doing all he could) "Do you think he is trying fairly hard to solve these problems or not hard at all?"

"How about the state government? Do you think they are trying as hard as they can to solve the main problems of cities like (Central City), or that they are not doing all they could to solve these problems?" (If not doing all they could) "Do you think they are trying fairly hard to solve these problems or not hard at all?"

"How about the federal government in Washington? Do you think they are trying as hard as they can to solve the main problems of cities like (Central City), or that they are not doing all they could to solve these problems?" (If not doing all they could) "Do you think they are trying fairly hard to solve these problems or not hard at all?"

set of institutions and officials but they are much more skeptical than whites. Data from the Kerner Commission report indicate that whites are more likely than blacks to respond favorably to questions about effectiveness of government performance at all levels of government. Table 2–7 summarizes some of these data.

A Summary: Linkages

This chapter has attempted to do three things: (1) to define public opinion, its attributes and character, (2) to discuss the major influences on the political socialization (that is, the formation of politically relevant opinions) of the public, and (3) to suggest the potential policy importance of public opinion.

The most generally important and interesting proposition

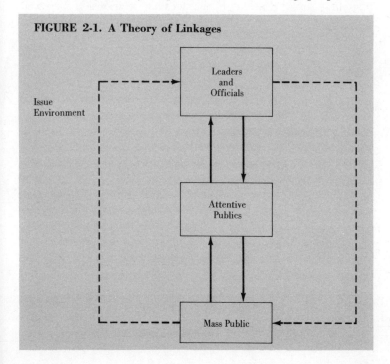

FIGURE 2-1. A Theory of Linkages

that emerges from this discussion is that attentive [23] publics and their opinions form an important link in many policy areas between leaders (officials) and the mass public and its opinions. A simplified view of the interaction is presented in Figure 2–1.

This diagram suggests that the most important relationships on any given issue are the ones between the attentive public and governmental leaders and between the attentive public and less interested or apathetic mass. The links between mass public and officials are less critical and less frequent.

In practice, there will be more than one of these opinion systems in operation at any one time (especially since there are many issues and different publics can form around them) and the membership of the attentive public certainly changes over time and over issues. But the notion of the linking between mass public, attentive public, and officials is a useful one for describing the real world. The links between elites and leaders operate strongly, although the weaker relationship between officials and mass public has received more attention in debates over democratic theory.

[23] The term "attentive" can encompass all the types of less-than-mass publics discussed earlier—special publics, interest groups, and so forth.

CHAPTER 3

Political Parties

Figure 2–1 is too simple: attentive publics do perform the vital linkage function described there, but political parties are also vital in understanding the linkage between citizens and government—between mass opinions and governmental policy statements and actions. Attentive publics work both in and through political parties, as well as apart from them. Some political-party activists are members of identifiable attentive publics; other political party activists are professionals more interested in gaining and retaining public offices than in transmitting opinions on specific issues. Some of the leaders and officials who receive this input from various publics are themselves affected by political parties—some belong to congressional parties; others are partisan in their beliefs and attitudes; others are partisan appointees. For purposes of including political parties, figure 2–1 should be revised as shown in Figure 3–1.

The link that parties help provide between the public and policies is imperfect and partial, but, especially through the

43

FIGURE 3-1. The Place of Political Parties in Policy and Opinion Linkage

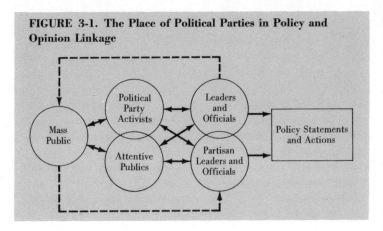

alternative candidates the parties offer for a whole range of national, state, and local offices, it is real. American parties are also extremely important inside the government in helping shape policy responses. It makes some difference, for example, which party controls the White House and Congress (this point will be explored in later chapters).

Political parties are ubiquitous phenomena in the American political system. They are present within the structure of government and outside of it. Parties have aspects that are real, tangible, and solid (formal organizations, meetings, chairmen) and aspects that are illusory and intangible (what does it mean to "belong" to the Republican or Democratic party?). Parties are truly national in scope (the terms Democrat and Republican are familiar all over the nation, although not everyone agrees what those terms mean); at the same time they are highly particularized regionally (the political behavior of Mississippi Democrats James Eastland and John Stennis and New York Democrat John Lindsay is not often similar).

Some claim it makes no difference which party wins an election because there is really no difference in parties anyway, yet we are confronted with the phenomenon of thousands of candidates running yearly for thousands of offices as if they mean it and as if they think it makes a difference who wins. At the same time millions of people bother to contribute to candidates, ring doorbells, stuff envelopes, and in other ways aid one party or the other; and many millions more at least take the trouble to vote. Apparently they too think that it makes some difference who wins.

At the opposite extreme of those who claim it makes no difference which party's candidates win are those who forecast doom for the Republic if any party other than their own wins. Yet, somehow the Republic continues; the losing candidates return to their normal pursuits as lawyers or businessmen unmolested and probably more visible in their professions simply because they ran, even though unsuccessfully.

National political parties are the least organized and weakest of all American party organizations, although they do provide choices for president that ultimately affect policy responses of government. In fact, organizationally, national parties barely exist—except for the quadrennial conventions and the rather feeble activities of the national committees during the other three years and fifty-one weeks, national parties can be viewed as mainly loose confederations of state and local parties, or as mental constructs, or as both.

State and local parties are much more organized than national parties. They not only provide candidates for state and local offices, they also nominate the candidates for Congress. Although a treatment of state and local parties is beyond the scope of this volume, their importance to national politics is evident in the following statement by Fred Greenstein:

> The state and local party systems, and the social forces that shape them, provide the base of American national-level party politics. Congress is staffed by men and women who are locally nominated and elected and who, in many cases, have made their way into politics at the lower governmental levels. The President is nominated by national convention delegates from the states and localities; state and local politicians man the wards and precincts in presidential elections.[1]

The major purpose of the two principal national parties is to win public offices. A number of smaller parties exist primarily to provide a forum for the expression of somewhat unusual and probably unpopular political opinions. If any of these

---

[1] Fred Greenstein, *The American Party System and the American People*, 2nd ed. (Englewood Cliffs, N.J.: Prentice-Hall, 1970), p. 86.

opinions begin to attract considerable public support one or both of the major parties will typically adopt at least part of this opinion as their own in order to siphon votes away from the minor party. Despite a variety of minor-party threats, since 1856 the same two parties (Democratic and Republican) have remained the major parties and have controlled both the White House and Congress without exception. Minor party candidacies have on occasion made some difference on which major party was victorious (particularly in presidential races) but no minor party has come even close to capturing the presidency and most have remained totally unrepresented in Congress. Since 1900, all minor parties combined have never had more than eighteen members of the House at any one time and they have never had more than four members of the Senate. Since 1940 third parties have almost entirely disappeared from Congress.

Despite the decentralization and lack of continuous organization that characterizes political parties at the national level, they do have important impact on society. They create a psychological involvement with politics on the part of the electorate, and they serve as a vehicle for actual political involvement. These features will be the subject of the remaining portions of this chapter. Subsequent chapters will discuss the impact of party politics on the conduct of public business by the president, Congress, and the federal courts.

Party Identification

Party membership in the United States is principally a state of mind—a matter of self identification. A few people join political clubs or organizations—Young Democrats, Young Republicans, and so on—but most who proclaim themselves to be Democrats or Republicans or Socialists or Prohibitionists have not "joined" any identifiable organization or have not paid dues to any one. Rather, they are simply proclaiming that they consider themselves to be Democrats or Republicans or Socialists or Prohibitionists.

Fortunately, we have good data over a reasonably long period of time on party identification—that is, how people say they feel about which party they "belong" to. In general, party identification over the last three decades has been reasonably stable, with a trend toward the Democrats that peaked in 1964 and then became stable at a somewhat lower level by 1967 and a simultaneous trend toward an increasing number of independents that peaked in 1967 and has remained at a high level since then. Figure 3–2 summarizes Gallup-poll data since 1940 on whether people consider themselves Republicans, Democrats or independents. Since 1964 the most interesting trend has been increasing identification with independents. And, in the latest poll available at the time of this writing (autumn, 1971), the independents have also gained at the expense of the Republicans. In fact, as of that poll, they outnumber the Republicans, as they had done off and on since 1967.

The move toward increased preference for independent status has been accentuated by the stated preference of newly enfranchised eighteen-, nineteen-, and twenty-year-olds who were eligible to vote for the first time in the 1972 presidential

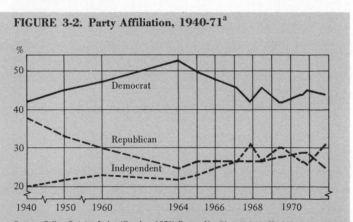

FIGURE 3-2. Party Affiliation, 1940-71[a]

Source: *Gallup Opinion Index* (October, 1971) Report No. 76, pp 22-23. Used by permission of the American Institute of Public Opinion (The Gallup Poll).

[a]This sample includes only those who were 21 and older.

TABLE 3-1. Distribution of Party Identification, 1952-1970

Party Identification	1952	1954	1956	1958	1960	1962	1964	1966	1968	1970
Strong Republican	13%	13%	15%	13%	14%	12%	11%	10%	9%	9%
Weak Republican	14%	14%	14%	16%	13%	16%	13%	15%	14%	15%
Independent Republican	7%	6%	8%	4%	7%	6%	6%	7%	9%	8%
Independent	5%	7%	9%	8%	8%	8%	8%	12%	10%	13%
Independent Democrat	10%	9%	7%	7%	8%	8%	9%	9%	10%	10%
Weak Democrat	25%	25%	23%	24%	25%	23%	25%	27%	26%	23%
Strong Democrat	22%	22%	21%	23%	21%	23%	26%	18%	20%	21%
Apolitical; Do Not Know	4%	4%	3%	5%	4%	4%	2%	2%	2%	1%

Source: Fred Greenstein, *The American Party System and the American People*, 2nd ed. (Englewood Cliffs, N.J.: Prentice-Hall, 1970), p. 37. Nineteen seventy figures compiled from Survey Research Center (University of Michigan) data.

election. In October, 1971, among those twenty-one and older, forty-five percent were Democrats, twenty-seven percent were Republicans, and twenty-eight percent were independents. Of the eighteen-, nineteen-, and twenty-year-olds polled at the same time, thirty-five percent called themselves Democrats, fourteen percent called themselves Republicans, and fifty-one percent called themselves independents.[2]

The Survey Research Center at the University of Michigan has been systematically sampling a representative proportion of the population at regular intervals for more than twenty years. The questions they ask about party identification allow for a more elaborate response in attempting to tap the intensity of partisan feelings, as well as the basic direction of party leaning. Table 3–1 summarizes SRC data on party identification at two-year intervals since 1952. These data have been collapsed (strong and weak Democrats, strong and weak Republicans, independents, independent Republicans, and independent Democrats) and graphed in Figure 3–3 to allow more ready comparison with Gallup findings. Figure 3–3 shows the same

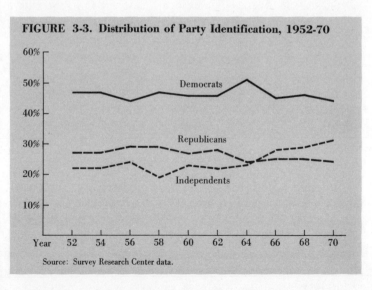

FIGURE 3-3. Distribution of Party Identification, 1952-70

Source: Survey Research Center data.

[2] *Gallup Opinion Index*, report no. 76 (October, 1971), p. 21.

basic trends as the Gallup data: relative stability for Democrats and Republicans in relation to each other (with Democrats outnumbering Republicans by a ratio of about 5 to 3) and a steady increase in the percent of independents. Since the Survey Research Center only conducts its interviews every two years these data do not reflect the recent trends in party identification that appear in the Gallup data.

Functions of Party Identification

In addition to strongly influencing electoral choice, party identification in general serves an important function by providing a perceptual screen for individuals through which they can view political objects. One's partisan orientation strongly influences one's outlook toward political phenomena. The national political landscape is very complex and far removed from the ordinary citizen, hence he needs to rely on secondary sources to provide information he can understand about matters in which he cannot participate directly. Identification with a political party serves this function and is, therefore, an opinion-shaping agent of great importance. Campbell and others have pointed out that "the strength of the relationship between party identification and dimensions of partisan attitude suggests that responses to each element of national politics are deeply affected by the individual's enduring party attachments."[3]

Campbell and his colleagues also discuss another impact of party identification: the strong association between the individual's attachment to a party and the degree of his psychological involvement in political affairs. A person who has formed a strong self-identification with one of the parties is much more likely to be interested in political affairs and to participate in them than someone who does not have such an identification.[4] However, it is not clear that party identification "causes" active participation. The association is a two way relationship, with each factor influencing the other.

[3] Angus Campbell, Philip E. Converse, Warren E. Miller, and Donald E. Strokes, *The American Voter*, abridged ed. (New York: Wiley, 1964), p. 73.

[4] *Ibid.*, p. 83.

Strength of party identification is thus a good clue both to strength and direction of political beliefs and to level of participation. The most strongly identified party members are the most likely to be very active in politics and to hold definite political views on issues. Their views will accord in general with common perceptions of the party's position, even though the party as such may not really have taken a position. On many issues the party's position is, in fact, the views of the strongest party identifiers. But these views have some coherence because the strongest party identifiers tend to agree with each other. It should also be noted that most office holders—both public offices and party offices—are among the strongest party identifiers. Therefore, the party's ideology tends to be self-perpetuating: those who subscribe to it most strongly are those who hold its most important positions and are, therefore, in a position to make official statements on the party's position.

Individuals with weaker party identification are more likely to hold views divergent from what is commonly held to be the party's position. They are less willing to become actively involved in the party's affairs.

Demographic Factors and Party Identification

In general, members of the less well-off classes tend to identify themselves as Democrats; members of the more well-off classes tend to identify themselves as Republicans. Table 3–2 shows a breakdown of party identifiers into several demographic categories for two presidential elections, 1952 and 1968. Although the percentages change slightly from year to year, the general trends are consistent. The table shows that the percent of Democratic identifiers exceeds the percent of Republican identifiers in lower-education categories; in higher-education categories, the percent of Republican identifiers exceeds Democratic identifiers. Blacks identify as Democrats more than as Republicans. Democratic identification is higher than Republican identification in lower-income groups; in higher-income groups, Republican identification is higher.

TABLE 3-2. Party Identification and Demographic Characteristics

	1952			1968		
	Democrats	Republicans	(N)	Democrats	Republicans	(N)
Education						
Grade School	51%	23%	(632)	67%	21%	(328)
High School	47%	28%	(708)	60%	29%	(712)
College	33%	38%	(237)	44%	46%	(392)
Age						
Less than 25 Years	57%	15%	(100)	61%	22%	(107)
25-34 Years	48%	21%	(383)	53%	35%	(290)
35-64 Years	46%	29%	(894)	58%	32%	(798)
65 Years or Older	42%	32%	(208)	57%	34%	(242)
Race						
White	46%	29%	(1445)	50%	37%	(1198)
Black	51%	12%	(157)	90%	4%	(229)
Religion						
Protestant	44%	32%	(1151)	54%	35%	(1054)
Catholic	56%	18%	(340)	66%	24%	(298)
Sex						
Male	46%	26%	(734)	56%	34%	(619)
Female	47%	28%	(872)	58%	30%	(822)
Income						
$0-4999	50%	24%	(1161)	62%	25%	(445)
$5000-9999	43%	33%	(353)	57%	32%	(547)
$10000-14999	17%	47%	(60)	58%	33%	(272)
$15000 or higher[a]				37%	51%	(147)

Source: Figures calculated from data provided by the Survey Research Center (University of Michigan).

[a] This was not a discrete category in the 1952 survey.

Political Participation

A very small part of the adult population actively works for a party or candidates in elections; a larger proportion engages in less demanding kinds of partisan activities. There are many different types of citizen participation that can take place in the United States. Some political participation, particularly in recent years, is not focused on political parties and is not of the traditional campaign-related type of activity. A variety of direct action, ranging from quiet sit-ins in the early 1960s though various-sized, well-ordered demonstrations to full-scale urban riots, all have political implications. The smaller, well-planned and executed demonstrations are explicitly political and those who participate are generally aware of the political ends they are seeking. The larger, less well-planned, and unfocused demonstrations, especially those that for one reason or another result in violence, are probably variously regarded by the participants. Some, no doubt, view them as political events and are clear about their political motivations for participation; others probably have very little awareness of any political motivation for participating and attach little political significance to their actions. These direct action phenomena deserve systematic study that has not yet been given them. Nevertheless, these activities are likely to remain less important in relation to policy responses than the more traditional campaign-oriented kinds of activities that have been systematically studied.

Lester Milbrath has studied political participation and has suggested a hierarchy of activities along a dimension of involvement ranging from apathy at the low end to holding public and party office at the high end.[5] An adaptation of Milbrath's scheme is presented in Figure 3–4.

There are several observations that can be made about political participation. As Figure 3–4 shows, the levels of activity tend to form clusters—at the bottom of the hierarchy are those

[5] Lester W. Milbrath, *Political Participation* (Chicago: Rand McNally, 1965), pp. 16–21.

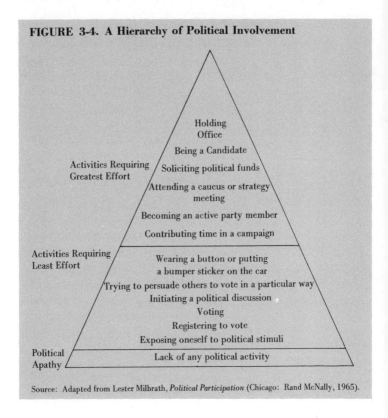

FIGURE 3-4. A Hierarchy of Political Involvement

Holding
Office

Being a Candidate

Soliciting political funds

Attending a caucus or strategy
meeting

Becoming an active party member

Contributing time in a campaign

Activities Requiring
Greatest Effort

Activities Requiring
Least Effort

Wearing a button or putting
a bumper sticker on the car

Trying to persuade others to vote in a particular way

Initiating a political discussion

Voting

Registering to vote

Exposing oneself to political stimuli

Political
Apathy

Lack of any political activity

Source: Adapted from Lester Milbrath, *Political Participation* (Chicago: Rand McNally, 1965).

who are apathetic and do not participate at all, in the middle area are those who participate minimally, and at the top those who participate actively.

A person's participatory role tends to be stable.[6] Activists tend to remain activist, and the apathetic tend to remain apathetic. Occasionally transition from apathy to minimal involvement or from minimal involvement to activism (or in the reverse direction) may occur, but a fairly strong stimulus from the environment is usually required to change a stable pattern of participation.

Understandably, the proportion of people who engage in different kinds of political activity decreases as the effort re-

[6] *Ibid.*, p. 20.

TABLE 3-3. Political Participation, 1952-68

Activity	1952	1956	1960	1964	1968
Registered to Vote	NA[a]	75%	78%	82%	83%
Read Something about the Presidential Campaign in the Newspaper	79%	69%	80%	79%	74%
Voted in Current Election	73%	73%	74%	78%	73%
Read Regularly about the Campaign (1952: Quite a Lot)	39%	NA	43%	40%	35%
Very Much Interested in Campaign	38%	38%	30%	37%	39%
Talked and Tried to Persuade Someone to Vote in a Particular Way	27%	28%	33%	31%	32%
Wrote to a Public Official expressing an Opinion	NA	NA	NA	17%	19%
Wore Campaign Button; Displayed Bumper Sticker	4%	10%	12%	11%	14%
Attended a Political Meeting, Rally, or Dinner during Campaign	7%	10%	8%	9%	9%
Belongs to a Political Club or Organization	2%	3%	3%	4%	4%
Wrote a Letter to the Editor Expressing a Political Opinion	NA	NA	NA	3%	2%

Source: National surveys conducted by the Survey Research Center (University of Michigan). The data for 1952-64 appeared in Fred Greenstein, *The American Party System and the American People*, 2nd ed. (Englewood Cliffs, N.J.: Prentice-Hall, 1970), p. 11. Nineteen sixty-eight data were calculated from data provided by the Survey Research Center (University of Michigan).

[a]not available

quired increases. Data on political participation in presidential election years summarized in Table 3–3 indicate that up to three-quarters of the population engage in some kind of activity that requires only minimal effort (voting, registering to vote) while less than one-twentieth engage in activities requiring a great amount of effort. In addition, activity tends to be cumulative, so that those people who are activist (for example, those who belong to political clubs or work in campaigns) also perform the activities in the middle of the hierarchy (registering, voting, keeping up with the campaign).

EXPLAINING POLITICAL PARTICIPATION: DEMOGRAPHIC FACTORS

Participation varies according to education, income, occupation, age, race, and other factors. In general, the more well-off are more active, the less well-off are less active, regardless of the type of activity. Also, as the degree of difficulty of activity increases, participation by the less well-off decreases. These generalizations are supported by data appearing in Table 3–4 on participation in the 1968 election.

EXPLAINING POLITICAL PARTICIPATION: PERSONAL FACTORS

A variety of personal factors are associated with political participation. In general, participation is higher when psychological involvement is high, cynicism is low, sense of citizen duty is high, perceived importance of the election is high, perceived difference in alternatives is high, and feelings of efficacy are high.[7] When psychological involvement is low, cynicism is high, sense of citizen duty is low, perceived importance of the election is low, perceived difference in alternatives is low, and feelings of efficacy are low, participation is likely to be low. Not surprisingly, these factors and the demographic factors discussed in the preceding section are closely related. That is, the more well-off are likely to be more psychologically involved than the less well-off, and so on.

[7] *Ibid.*, pp. 51–64.

TABLE 3-4. Political Participation and Demography, 1968

	Education			Income				Age				Sex		Race	
	Grade School	High School	College	$0-4999	$5000-9999	$10000-14999	>$15000[a]	≤$24[b]	25-34	35-64	≥65	Male	Female	White	Black
Registered to Vote															
Yes	77%	84%	87%	74%	85%	90%	93%	55%	78%	88%	85%	86%	81%	85%	77%
No	22%	16%	13%	26%	15%	9%	7%	44%	22%	11%	15%	14%	18%	15%	22%
Voted															
Yes	59%	75%	83%	59%	76%	82%	90%	51%	71%	78%	70%	75%	72%	75%	64%
No	39%	24%	16%	39%	23%	14%	10%	49%	28%	20%	29%	22%	27%	23%	34%
Read Something about Campaign															
Yes	59%	73%	91%	63%	78%	84%	87%	63%	74%	77%	71%	78%	71%	76%	66%
No	41%	27%	9%	37%	22%	16%	13%	37%	26%	23%	29%	22%	29%	27%	35%
Talked and Persuaded															
Yes	22%	31%	44%	23%	33%	42%	41%	30%	36%	33%	27%	40%	27%	32%	33%
No	78%	69%	56%	77%	67%	59%	59%	69%	64%	67%	73%	60%	73%	68%	66%
Worked for a Candidate or Party															
Yes	2%	5%	9%	3%	6%	7%	9%	3%	5%	6%	5%	5%	6%	6%	3%
No	96%	94%	91%	96%	94%	92%	91%	96%	95%	93%	93%	94%	93%	93%	96%
(N) =	(328)	(712)	(392)	(445)	(547)	(272)	(147)	(107)	(290)	(798)	(242)	(619)	(822)	(1198)	(229)

Source: Figures calculated from data provided by the Survey Research Center (University of Michigan).
a. The symbol ≥ means equal to or greater than.
b. The symbol ≤ means equal to or less than.

57

EXPLAINING POLITICAL PARTICIPATION: EXPOSURE TO POLITICAL STIMULI

Political participation increases as exposure to political stimuli increases. People who have been contacted by a party worker, who read about the campaign, and who talk to their friends about political matters are more likely to be politically active than those who are not exposed to political stimuli. In addition to the correlation between high socioeconomic status and exposure to political stimuli, one's interest in politics, family influence, and strength of political preference are also related to exposure to political stimuli.[8]

PARTY VOTING IN THE ELECTORATE

Voting tends to be consonant with party identification, but there is enough slippage to allow the minority party to win some of the time. The general characteristics of Democratic and Republican voters are similar to those of persons who identify themselves as Democrats and Republicans. Thus, in general, the less well-off tend to vote Democratic, and the more well-off tend to vote Republican. This is evident from Table 3–5, which presents the demographic characteristics of the electorate in two presidential elections.

The table shows first of all that 1952 was an unusual election because of the great appeal of the Republican candidate that caused many voters to abandon their traditional party identification and vote for Eisenhower. In subsequent elections, more traditional voting alignments have returned: Democrats have tended to receive support from the blacks, the less educated, the poorer, and the Catholics, while Republicans have tended to receive support from the highly educated, those with higher incomes, Protestants, and older groups. 1972 was another exceptional election: distrust of the Democratic presidential candidate led many normal Democratic voters either not to vote or to vote for the incumbent Republican President.

It is also clear from the table that nonvoting is more likely to occur in the same groups from which the Democrats draw

[8] These findings are discussed in *ibid.*, pp. 39–47.

TABLE 3-5. Voting and Demography

	1952				1968			
	Voting Democratic	Voting Republican	Not Voting	(N)	Voting Democratic	Voting Republican	Not Voting	(N)
Education								
Grade Scool	30%	32%	37%	(632)	32%	18%	39%	(328)
High School	34%	46%	20%	(708)	34%	32%	24%	(712)
College	24%	65%	11%	(237)	30%	47%	16%	(392)
Age								
Less than 25 Years	24%	32%	44%	(100)	22%	23%	49%	(107)
25 - 34 years	32%	38%	29%	(383)	31%	30%	28%	(290)
35 - 64 years	32%	45%	22%	(894)	34%	35%	20%	(798)
65 years or older	26%	46%	27%	(208)	32%	36%	29%	(242)
Race								
White	31%	46%	22%	(1445)	27%	39%	23%	(1198)
Black	26%	6%	67%	(157)	61%	2%	34%	(229)
Religion								
Protestant	26%	45%	29%	(1151)	28%	36%	26%	(1054)
Catholic	43%	41%	16%	(340)	44%	28%	22%	(298)
Union Member								
Yes	42%	33%	24%	(437)	38%	26%	24%	(346)
No	26%	46%	27%	(1169)	31%	35%	25%	(1080)
Income								
$0 - 4999	32%	37%	30%	(1161)	29%	23%	39%	(445)
$5000 - 9999	30%	56%	14%	(353)	33%	34%	23%	(547)
$10000 - 14999	22%	73%	5%	(60)	40%	36%	14%	(272)
More than $15000[a]					27%	54%	10%	(147)

Source: Figures calculated from data provided by the Survey Research Center (University of Michigan).
a. This was not a discrete category in the 1952 survey.

support: the less educated, the younger, and the poorer. This poses a challenge for Democrats as they map strategies for winning elections: they must mobilize the segments of society that support them in principle, but that are unlikely to vote unless directly stimulated. This point is borne out by comparing data in Table 3–2 and Table 3–5. The proportion of people in various social groups identifying themselves as Democrats is much higher than the proportion in the same social groups who actually voted for the Democratic candidate. The proportion of those identifying themselves as Republicans is much closer to the proportion of those who voted Republican. (The exception in 1952 can be explained by the candidate's personal appeal.) In part this is a function of the fact that Democrats' support lies in those social groups least likely to vote, but it is also an indication that party identification does not bind a person to vote, nor does it bind a person to vote in a particular way. It is clear that when the decision time comes, factors other than simple party identification are considered by the voter. But party identification is still the best predictor of vote that exists. Chapter 4 will deal with some of the factors that bear upon the political act of voting.

It is evident from Table 3–5 that both parties pull votes from all groups. While one party may be stronger among certain groups than the other party, there is not any control of votes by either party. This lack of dominance of social groups makes inappropriate a strict class interpretation of American electoral politics.

There is some evidence to suggest that traditional alignments and voting habits may be shifting. The increased number of citizens identifying themselves as independents may indicate a trend toward increased emphasis on the evaluation of the candidate and decreased emphasis on party voting. The 1972 returns suggest support for this point—the incumbent Republican president won an overwhelming victory, but in senatorial, congressional, gubernatorial, and various state and local elections the Democrats did quite well.

Table 3–6 suggests a second possible trend that may alter some of the patterns described above. Two things can be

TABLE 3-6. Blue-Collar and White-Collar Voting in the 1968 Election

Blue-Collar[a]Whites	Nixon	Humphrey	Wallace
21 - 24[b]	48%	19%	33%
25 - 34	40%	23%	37%
35 - 64	31%	50%	19%
White-Collar Whites			
21 - 24[b]	43%	45%	12%
25 - 34	52%	34%	14%
35 - 64	57%	30%	13%

Source: Opinion Research Corporation, Princeton, N.J. These data appeared in Michael Rappeport, "Party Alignment: The Biggest Shift in Forty Years," *The Washington Monthly*, vol. 3 (November, 1971), p. 20. Reprinted with permission from *The Washington Monthly*, November 1971. Copyright 1971 by The Washington Monthly Company, 1150 Conn. Ave. N.W., Washington, D.C. 20036.

a. Blue collar is defined as the census categories of craftsmen and foremen, operatives, service workers, and laborers. White collar similarly as professional, managerial, and sales workers. Occupation is assigned on the basis of husband in husband-wife family.
b. Students are omitted.

noted about the voting of blue-collar and white-collar workers in 1968: the plurality that Nixon enjoyed in the under-35, blue-collar group, and the great attractiveness of George Wallace in the same age group. Assuming that when the Wallace phenomenon disappears about half of the Wallace votes will go back to the Republicans and half to the Democrats, then the Republicans will come away with a healthy majority in at least this generation of blue-collar workers. What is unsure, however, is how the Wallace voters will react if their candidate disappears from the active political scene. Since most of them would come from normally Democratic backgrounds, a large majority of them may return to the Democratic fold or may simply quit voting. In this case the emerging Republican majority among blue-collar workers might turn out to be illusory.

The 1972 election, at least at the presidential level, suggests that changes are continuing to occur although the permanence of them is certainly in question. Table 3-7 summarizes the results of the presidential elections of 1956 and 1972, using a number of categories similar to those in Table 3-5. A com-

TABLE 3-7. Voting for President, 1956 and 1972

	1956		1972	
	Voting Demo-cratic	Voting Repub-lican	Voting Demo-cratic	Voting Repub-lican
Education				
Grade School	50%	50%	49%	51%
High School	42%	58%	34%	66%
College	31%	69%	37%	63%
Age				
Under 30 years	43%	57%	48%	52%
30 - 49 years	45%	55%	33%	67%
50 years or older	39%	61%	36%	64%
Race				
White	41%	59%	32%	68%
Nonwhite	61%	39%	87%	13%
Religion				
Protestant	37%	63%	30%	70%
Catholic	51%	49%	48%	52%
Occupation				
Professional and				
Business	32%	68%	31%	69%
White Collar	37%	63%	36%	64%
Manual (Blue Collar)	50%	50%	43%	57%
Members of Labor				
Union Families	57%	43%	46%	54%
Party				
Republican	4%	96%	5%	95%
Democratic	85%	15%	67%	33%
Independent	30%	70%	31%	69%

Source: Adapted from data appearing in *Gallup Opinion Index* (December, 1972), p. 10.

parison of the 1972 data in Table 3–7 with the data in Table 3–5 supports the generalization that every group was more heavily Republican than normal, with the single exception of nonwhite voters, who remained overwhelmingly Democratic.

Table 3–7 by itself, however, offers additional insight into the nature of the Nixon victory in 1972. Nineteen fifty-six was picked as the logical comparison because it was the only other Republican landslide on which data on the voting of specific socioeconomic groups are available. In some respects the 1956 Eisenhower victory and the 1972 Nixon victory look the same: those with grade-school educations, 50 years of age and older, Catholic in religion, either professional and business or white collar in occupation, Republican or independent in party identification all voted in 1972 virtually as they had in 1956 (no more than three percentage points difference being defined as lack of change). The Democratic candidate in 1972, George McGovern, actually did better than the Democratic candidate in 1956, Adlai Stevenson, among nonwhite voters, voters under 30, and college-educated voters.

The Republican candidate in 1972, however, improved significantly on the 1956 Republican performance among those with high-school educations, between 30 and 49, white, Protestant, engaged in manual labor (including those belonging to labor unions), and Democrats. In short, the magnitude of the Nixon victory can be explained by a very large defection among normally Democratic voters—especially high-school educated, white, Protestant workers in their 30s and 40s. Obviously, if these voters remain Republican in presidential voting, the Democratic party is in trouble. They cannot hope to offset such losses by continuing gains among nonwhites, those under 30, and those with college educations. A winning electoral coalition cannot be based on those groups alone, as George McGovern and the Democrats should have found out convincingly in 1972.

CHAPTER 4

Voting and Elections

Elections are highly visible occasions in American political life through which voters can directly accept or reject candidates nominated by political parties for public office and can indirectly express their opinions on the past conduct of public affairs and their hopes for future conduct. The two kinds of national elections, presidential and congressional (for members of the House and Senate), will be the focus of this chapter.

Presidential elections are in many way the grandest arena of American politics. The most powerful office in the nation and probably the world is at stake. It is the single most consistently visible, recurring political event in the life of the nation. Because the course of policy is altered by this choice, voters are in a position to influence policy even though in imperfect and, in part, partially unforeseen ways.

Congressional elections are considerably less visible than presidential elections. Any single Senate seat or House seat may not be perceived to be terribly critical. Turnout is considerably lower and so is interest. In these elections, taken singly, the voter is having a considerably less direct say about the course of policy than in a presidential election (thus, it is "logical" that turnout is higher in presidential elections). The cumulative results, however, have a great deal to do with policy, because they determine which party and which part of which party is in control in Congress. But any single voter does not, except in the abstract sense, help make the cumulative choice.

Voting Turnout

PRESIDENTIAL ELECTIONS

As Table 4-1 shows, voting turnout for presidental elections was fairly stable between 1952 and 1968, fluctuating between sixty percent and sixty-five perecnt of those of voting age. The changes from election to election were not dramatic, although each percentage point represents about a million

TABLE 4-1. Turnout in Presidential and Congressional Elections, 1952-70

Year	Presidential Turnout	Congressional Turnout
1952	62.6%	58.6%
1954	————	42.4%
1956	60.1%	56.6%
1958	————	43.4%
1960	64.0%	59.6%
1962	————	46.7%
1964	62.9%	58.7%
1966	————	46.3%
1968	61.8%	55.8%
1970	————	44.4%
1972	55.0%	NA[a]

Source: *Statistical Abstract of the United States, 1970*, p. 368. *Statistical Abstract of the United States, 1971*, p. 366. Data for 1972 based on unofficial returns.

[a]not available

people. But the trend since 1960 has been toward steadily decreasing interest in voting for president, especially in non-southern states.[1] This trend was underscored in 1972 when the presidential contest attracted only fifty-five percent of the eligible voters. The decline in turnout is also evident when one compares the number of potential voters (that is, those adults old enough to vote) to the number that actually voted. In 1960, there were 83.6 million potential voters (that is, those satisfying various state residency requirements) and 58.3 million of them voted (sixty-nine percent). In 1964 there 86.7 million potential voters and 58.0 million of them voted (sixty-seven percent). In 1968 there were 91.0 million potential voters and 58.2 million of them voted (sixty-four percent).

The point has already been made that persons from higher socioeconomic backgrounds are more likely to vote than persons from lower socioeconomic backgrounds. Education is an especially important factor related to voting turnout (see Table 3–5). Age is also an important factor: in general, younger adults vote less often than older ones do. This trend may be partly offset as the level of education in the population increases, especially among young people who are attending college in ever increasing numbers (in 1970, for example, fifty percent of white males twenty to twenty-one had some college; forty-one percent of those twenty-two to twenty-four had some college; thirty-seven percent of those twenty-five to thirty-four had some college; and only twenty-five percent of those forty-five to fifty-four had some college).

CONGRESSIONAL ELECTIONS

Table 4–1 also shows the data on turnout for congressional elections (for members of the House of Representatives). Several facts are evident from this table: first, turnout for congressional elections is always lower than turnout for presidential elections. But the level of turnout varies—it is higher in years when a presidential candidate is also on the ticket,

---

[1] Michael Rappeport, "Party Alignment: The Biggest Shift in Forty Years," *The Washington Monthly*, vol. 3 (November, 1971), pp. 19–21.

but it still runs about five percent below the turnout for president. (That a voter on election day in a presidential election year may be in the voting booth and vote for president but not for congressman illustrates the generally lower visibility of congressional elections and suggests the problems that congressional candidates face as they run for office.) Only about forty-five percent of the voters vote for members of the House when the presidency is not at stake.

Turnout in congressional elections is also related to socioeconomic class and age. As in presidential elections, the more well-off the potential voter is and the older he is (up to retirement age), the more likely he is to vote.

Turnout for congressional elections varies widely between individual contests on the same election day. An uncontested race or virtually uncontested race in a rural congressional district may attract only ten percent or fifteen percent of the eligible voters, whereas a hotly contested race in a suburban area may draw seventy percent or eighty percent of the voters.

Factors Affecting Voting

Motivation

When we speak of potential voters and actual voters, the question naturally arises, what is the difference between a voter and a nonvoter? How can we account for turnout versus nonturnout? Exogenous factors play some role: a flat tire, bad weather, or poor health may prevent a citizen from voting. But such factors account for only a small percent of nonvoters. Furthermore, they all assume that the citizen was already predisposed to vote. More useful explanatory factors are those that tap the motivation to vote at all.

The importance of socioeconomic status (SES) in affecting turnout has already been suggested. The components of SES—education, income, occupation—vary directly with turnout: as SES increases, turnout increases.

The intensity of partisan preference also helps explain turnout. People who identify themselves as *strong* Republicans

67

or Democrats are more likely to vote than those who have a weaker party identification.[2]

The level of turnout is also affected by the sense of political involvement experienced by the electorate (political involvement is a term used by Campbell and his colleagues to describe a voter's psychological identification with politics). There are several components of political involvement—interest in the campaign, concern over the outcome of the election, sense of political efficacy (a feeling that one can have an impact in the political system, that one's political behavior is in the long run important and functional), and sense of citizen duty. These factors are fairly highly correlated with each other, and with SES, and they are directly related to the likelihood of turnout: the higher the campaign interest, concern over election outcome, sense of political efficacy, and sense of citizen duty, the higher the turnout is likely to be.[3] It is also true that the lower the sense of political involvement, the lower the turnout is likely to be.

CANDIDATE CHOICE

Given a predisposition on the part of a citizen to vote, what factors account for the way he votes?

Party identification is a very important explanatory factor, as was suggested in Chapter 3. When all else is in a state of confusion, one can always rely on partisan preference to serve as a reference point in deciding about the candidate for whom one should vote. This becomes truer as the level of the information about a candidate decreases. However, all persons do not claim to identify with a party, and some identify only weakly.

The level of information about the candidates to which the voter is exposed also also helps determine his vote. There are many different sources of information and not all people are exposed to the same sources and in the same degree, nor do

[2] Angus Campbell, Philip E. Converse, Warren E. Miller, and Donald E. Stokes, *The American Voter*, abridged ed. (New York: Wiley, 1964), pp. 52–54.

[3] *Ibid.*, pp. 55–60.

they filter information the same way. Political campaigns obviously provide a major source of information that is purveyed through the media: television, radio, newspapers, and magazines. These sources form the factual basis for much political discussion that occurs in social settings, between friends, family members, and co-workers. (This social interaction itself is an important additional source of information—informed people can interact with uninformed people and serve as sources of information.) Not surprisingly, exposure to sources of information is directly related to socioeconomic status: the higher the SES, the more likely a person is to be informed, to read, and to discuss political matters.

A final and very important set of decision factors are the voters' attitudes toward the candidates and the issues. Campbell and his colleagues derived an attitudinal component analysis to measure the attitudinal forces influencing presidential vote choice. Essentially they decomposed an election outcome into a set of attitude components.[4] The analysis employs six components: image of Republican candidate, image of Democratic candidate, group-related attitudes, and attitudes toward party performance, domestic policy, and foreign policy. Figure 4–1 portrays four presidential elections using the attitudinal analysis scheme. The bar graphs suggest the relative weight and direction of each set of attitudes. Several general statements are suggested by the figure. First, it is normal for group-related attitudes and domestic policy preferences to favor the Democrats. Second, it is normal for party performance and foreign policy preferences to favor the Republicans. Third, both Republican and Democratic candidates usually have a generally favorable image that helps their candidacy and attracts votes. The 1964 election is clearly abnormal in that every factor, including Republican image, pushed in the direction of the Democrats.

The preceding discussion has been based on research dealing with presidential elections and turnout. Less empirical work on congressional elections and turnout has been done. It seems

[4] *Ibid.*, pp. 270–273.

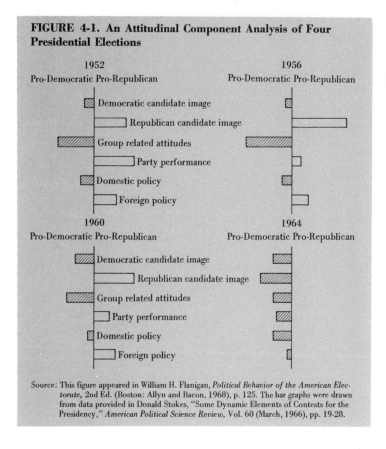

FIGURE 4-1. An Attitudinal Component Analysis of Four Presidential Elections

Source: This figure appeared in William H. Flanigan, *Political Behavior of the American Electorate*, 2nd Ed. (Boston: Allyn and Bacon, 1968), p. 125. The bar graphs were drawn from data provided in Donald Stokes, "Some Dynamic Elements of Contests for the Presidency," *American Political Science Review*, Vol. 60 (March, 1966), pp. 19-28.

likely, however, that most of the factors at work in presidential elections also appear in congressional elections, although to a lesser degree. Some hypotheses about voting in congressional elections can be ventured at this point:

—the stronger the partisan preference, the more likely the voter will turn out;

—the higher the socioeconomic status, the more likely the voter will turn out;

—the higher the sense of political involvement, the more likely the voter will turn out;

—given the lower visibility of congressional candidates and

elections, reliance on party identification as a decision factor is probably greater than in presidential elections;

—given the general inability of the population to link specific congressional candidates with specific policy stands, it seems likely that the candidate images, group-related attitudes, and general images of the two parties are likely to explain more of congressional voting than domestic and foreign-policy considerations.

The Time of Voter Decision

In a presidential election about one-fifth to one-third of the electorate reports making up its mind during the campaign; this means that close contests can be decided by changes of mind that take place during and perhaps because of the campaign. Most presidential voters make up their minds before the campaign even begins. But the one-third to one-fifth who report making up their minds during the campaign can make a critical difference. For example, in 1968 there is good evidence from the polls that enough people were swinging toward Democrat Hubert Humphrey to bring him very close to Republican Richard Nixon in the final balloting; if the election had been a week later and the trend had continued, Humphrey probably would have become President instead of Nixon.

Table 4–2 summarizes the data on time of decision in presidential elections. Nineteen fifty-six stands out as an exceptional year because everyone knew that Dwight Eisenhower would be the Republican nominee, and most knew whether they would vote for or against Eisenhower before the conventions.

Less is known about the time of decision in congressional campaigns. Given the lower visibility of congressional elections and candidates in general, it seems reasonable to assume that a smaller percentage of the votes are changed by the congressional campaign than are changed by the presidential campaign. There is, of course, some spillover ("coattail effect") from the presidential campaign into at least some congressional and senatorial contests, although this effect varies greatly from

TABLE 4-2. Time of Vote Choice for President

	1948	1952	1956	1960	1964	1968
Decided						
Before Conventions	37%	34%	57%	30%	40%	33%
During Conventions	28%	31%	18%	30%	25%	22%
During Campaign	25%	31%	21%	36%	33%	38%
Don't Remember; No Answer	10%	4%	4%	4%	3%	7%
Total	100%	100%	100%	100%	101%[a]	100%
(N) =	(424)	(1251)	(1285)	(1445)	(1126)	(1039)

Source: Survey Research Center (University of Michigan) data. This table appeared in William H. Flanigan, *Political Behavior of the American Electorate*, 2nd ed. (Boston: Allyn and Bacon, 1972), p. 109.
a. Adds to more than 100 because of rounding.

election to election. For example, the 1964 landslide for Lyndon Johnson also produced a lot of new Democrats in Congress; however, the 1972 Nixon landslide produced only a handful of new Republicans in the House and two fewer Republican senators.

Getting Elected: The Advantage of Incumbents

PRESIDENTIAL INCUMBENTS

An incumbent president is not assured of reelection if he seeks it, but he has an enormous advantage. The principal reason for this advantage is the news coverage afforded the president. He is on the front pages of newspapers and on television news programs day after day. He can preempt national television time at will. He is the symbol of the entire government for most citizens. He can dwarf the news coverage given any prospective opponent during most of his term; and even during the campaign he will continue to make news as president as well as a candidate. His opponent can make news only as a candidate.

The fact that he is president during a campaign allows the incumbent to time certain policy statements and actions to have a maximum desired political impact. For example, a few days before the 1968 election President Johnson ceased all bombing of North Vietnam. He was not running for reelection personally but the timing of the statement was clearly intended to aid the candidacy of the Democratic nominee, Hubert Humphrey. In 1972 the great flurry of activity in relation to peace in Vietnam that came in October seems to have been well-timed by the Nixon administration to dull that potentially harmful issue in the campaign.

Despite these enormous advantages, incumbents do lose. Since 1789 twenty-two presidents have sought reelection. Fifteen of these men succeeded; seven were defeated. Since the Civil War fourteen presidents have sought reelection, and only four failed to win. In the twentieth century, seven out of the nine men

73

THE ENVIRONMENT FOR GOVERNMENT ACTIVITY

who sought reelection won (and one of those men, Franklin Roosevelt, won three times). Only William Howard Taft in 1912 and Herbert Hoover in 1932 ran and were defeated.

CONGRESSIONAL INCUMBENTS

Incumbents in the House and Senate also have a great advantage in seeking to retain their seats. They may be unknown to a fair number of their constituents, but they are far more widely known than the challenging candidates. Thus, most incumbents win. Table 4–3 summarizes data on House and Senate incumbents' reelections. Between 1924 and 1956, an average of twenty percent of the members of any newly convened House were freshmen. (In the last few decades, however, this figure has declined to between ten and fifteen percent.) In the Senate, between 1946 and 1964, sixty percent of the incumbents have been returned from the average election; this means that usually there are only a dozen or so freshmen senators in any new Senate (because only one-third of the seats are up for election in any given even-numbered year). One reason the percentage of Senators running for reelection

TABLE 4-3. Reelection Record of Incumbent Officeholders

	U.S. Representatives (1924-56)	U.S. Senators (1946-64)
Percent Who Ran for Reelection	88%	76%
Percent of Those Who Ran Who Were Successful	90%	79%
Percent of Incumbents Returned to Office	79%	60%

Source: David A. Leuthold, *Electioneering in a Democracy* (New York: Wiley, 1968), p. 127.

TABLE 4-4. Percentage of Districts Won by Incumbent-Party Candidates (Incumbent Not Seeking Reelection)

Year	Total Districts	Won by Incumbent Party Candidate	Won by Challenger
1954	34	29 85.3%	5 14.7%
1956	32	26 81.3%	6 18.7%
1958	46	31 67.4%	15 32.6%
1960	37	26 70.3%	11 29.7%

Source: Charles O. Jones, "The Role of the Campaign in Congressional Politics," in M. Kent Jennings and Harmon Zeigler, *The Electoral Process* (Englewood Cliffs, N.J.: Prentice-Hall, 1966), p. 26.

is relatively low is that a fairly high proportion of incumbents die before the end of their six-year term.

Even in those districts and states in which the incumbent personally does not run, his party is usually successful in retaining his seat. Table 4–4 summarizes some data on the House of Representatives to support this point. Party turnover is more likely in the Senate. Between 1954 and 1968 the party of a retiring incumbent held the seat fifty-four percent of the time (twenty out of thirty-seven cases).

The Link between Elections and Policy Responses

PRESIDENTIAL ELECTIONS

Elections can serve as judgments of past policies, bestowing either approval (for example, 1964 and 1972) or disapproval (for example, 1932). In addition to this retrospective policy judgment, presidential elections afford the American electorate the opportunity to influence future policy in its general shape. Gerald Pomper has summarized this view:

> Given American institutions and voting behavior, ballots are unlikely to be means of direct control, but can be a method for indirect influence over policy. Elections are best considered as control mechanisms. In regard to policy, their principal function is to set boundaries—to provide legitimation for elite initiatives, to prevent actions which infringe on perceived vital interests, and to pass a retrospective judgment on these programs. Voting does not define the entire political system. It is one, but only one, vital input, an input most readily used by unorganized and unprivileged masses in attempts to gain attention to their needs and wants.[5]

There is considerable evidence that although American voters may not be well-informed on all of the details of presidential-candidates' positions and may not have thought through their own positions on a broad range of public issues, they still know enough about both the candidates' positions and their own positions to vote with a high degree of consistency for those candidates who do, in fact, most nearly espouse the positions on issues that they find appealing or congenial.

V. O. Key, after studying electoral and public opinion data for a twenty-five year period (1936–1960), reached the following conclusions: [6]

1. Supporters of the "ins" (the party controlling the presidency) who disagree with their policies are most likely to defect in a subsequent election. Supporters who agree with the policies of their party are most likely to continue voting for the candidates of that party.

2. Supporters of the "outs" who find their policies congenial are most likely to remain loyal. Those who have come to concur with the ins are most likely to defect.

---

[5] Gerald M. Pomper, "Control and Influence in American Elections," *American Behavioral Scientist*, vol. 13 (November/December, 1969), p. 217.

[6] These conclusions appear in V. O. Key, Jr., *The Responsible Electorate* (Cambridge: Harvard University Press, 1966), pp. 149–151.

3. There are some individuals ("standpatters") who stay with a party despite serious policy disagreements. But because policy preference reinforces party loyalty, those who agree with their party are most inclined to stay with it, while whose whose policy preferences conflict are most likely to defect.

4. There are also "switchers," who move between the parties in large numbers from election to election. They "evidently are not party stalwarts who rely on the leaders of their own party for their policy outlooks or their candidate preferences." [7]

In summary, Key says, "All these patterns of behavior are consistent with the supposition that voters, or at least a large number of them, are moved by their perceptions and appraisals of policy and performance. They like or do not like the performance of government." [8]

Nelson Polsby and Aaron Wildavsky, in a study of presidential elections,[9] have argued at length that the present presidential-election system allows for a reasonably good fit between public preferences and the choice of the candidate most likely to carry out those preferences. The key to their argument is that in the American political system coalitions must be formed in order to achieve anything. This is no less true of presidential-election politics than it is of nomination politics, legislative politics, or bureaucratic politics. Since there are only two major parties, both of them must seek to build a large coalition, and this inevitably means that the support of a large number of groups and individuals must be sought. The same issues do not interest all groups and individuals, and therefore both major-party candidates must take specific positions on a variety of issues that are only partially visible to a large segment of the electorate. In addition, of course, both major-party candidates must also take positions on the few major issues in any campaign that are visible to virtually all groups and potential voters.

[7] *Ibid.*, p. 151.

[8] *Ibid.*, p. 150.

[9] Nelson W. Polsby and Aaron Wildavsky, *Presidential Elections*, 3rd ed. ((New York: Scribners, 1971).

The argument presented by Polsby and Wildavsky is worth quoting at some length:

> It would be inaccurate to suggest that voters in presidential elections transmit their policy preferences with a high degree of reliability. There are few clear mandates in our political system owing to the fact that elections are fought on so many issues and in so many incompletely overlapping constituencies. . . .
>
> Presidential elections are not referenda. The relationship between Presidential elections and policies is a great deal subtler than the relations between the outcomes of referenda and the policies they pertain to. In theory, the American political system is designed to work like this: two teams of men, one in office, the other seeking office, both attempt to get enough votes to win elections. In order to win, they go to various groups of voters and, by offering to pursue policies favored by these groups, hope to attract their votes. If there were only one office-seeking team, their incentive to respond to the policy preferences of groups in the population would diminish; if there were many such teams, the chances that any one of them could achieve a sufficient number of backers to govern would diminish. Hence the two-party system is regarded as a kind of compromise between the goals of responsiveness and effectiveness.[10]

The authors continue:

> Free elections and a two-party system operate to bring governmental policy roughly in line with intense public preferences over a reasonable span of time. Through the trial and error of repeated electoral experiences, party leaders discover that certain policies must be excluded and others included if they are to have any hope of winning. The "out" party has a built-in incentive to propose policies more popular than the "in" party in order to assume office. And the "in" party is highly motivated to respond by adopting the policy itself or by proposing others which it believes may be even more popular. Party competition for votes brings public policy into accord with private preferences. This calculus of support is far from precise; it is necessarily based more on hunch and guesswork at any point in time than on hard facts.[11]

[10] *Ibid.*, p. 298–299.
[11] *Ibid.*, p. 309.

This view applies to many areas of public endeavor. It does seem to ignore, however, those areas in which the public is almost totally uninterested or which have not yet been put on the public's agenda in one way or another. In these areas political leaders and governmental officials create their own demand for certain kinds of policies by either proceeding on their own initiative or stimulating relevant policy elites to support what the leaders and officials think should be done. That is, numerous policy innovations are stimulated by the rulers, not the ruled. This may result in either wise or unwise policy, but it certainly suggests that not all major policy areas come within the constant purview of the electoral process.

CONGRESSIONAL ELECTIONS

In general, congressional elections taken singly have a lower issue content and less implication for policy change than presidential elections. The saliency of the candidates and the legislative records of the parties is very low in congressional election years. Stokes and Miller found that of the people in districts where the House seat was contested in 1958; fifty-nine percent said they had neither read nor heard anything about either candidate, and less than one in five felt that they knew something about both candidates. In addition, of the reasons respondents gave for their House vote in 1958, only about seven percent had discernible policy content.[12] In addition, only forty-seven percent of this sample was able to identify correctly which party was in control of Congress.[13]

Charles Jones has argued persuasively that the policy relevance of congressional elections is quite low, certainly less than that of presidential elections.[14] His principal argument is that the campaign and election serve as a time for the candidate to get elected rather than as a forum for the discussion of issues

[12] Donald E. Stokes and Warren E. Miller, "Party Government and the Saliency of Congress," *Public Opinion Quarterly*, vol. 26 (winter, 1962), p. 536.

[13] *Ibid.*

[14] Charles O. Jones, "The Role of the Campaign in Congressional Politics," in M. Kent Jennings and L. Harmon Zeigler, *The Electoral Process* (Englewood Cliffs, N.J.: Prentice-Hall, 1966), pp. 21–41.

and policy. He lists several supporting propositions and contingencies:

1. Elections are scheduled by the calendar—not by issue emergence.
2. An overwhelming majority of incumbents are returned to office.
3. Voters are almost totally unaware of issues in congressional elections, and a majority are unaware of the candidates.
4. The incumbent's campaign will be designed to identify him to as many voters as possible. His specific campaign activity and techniques will vary depending on the characteristics of his constituency. He will not be committed to specific issue stands during the campaign except by choice.
5. The victorious incumbent will not alter his policy-making behavior as a result of percentage changes at elections.[15]

Some congressional elections, however, have more room for policy impact than others. Specifically, elections in districts that are consistently highly competitive, in new (redistricted) districts, in highly urbanized districts, and in districts in which there is no incumbent often generate increased turnout and participation and, presumably, increased interest in issues.

Finally, it should also be noted that although individual congressional elections may not have much policy content, the policy impact of all House and Senate elections taken together is great because they determine which party and which part of which party controls Congress. And, in general, a Democratic Congress (particularly one with a large Democratic majority) will expand the domestic activities of the government and a Republican Congress will either contract those activities or maintain the existing situation.

The Future of American Elections

The normal majority in the United States in voting for both president and Congress is still Democratic, although the nature of that majority (particularly in presidential voting) has changed in recent years.

[15] *Ibid.*, p. 38.

The data presented in Chapter 3 details the nature and stability of party identification in the United States. The relative position of the two parties has remained quite constant for the last several decades and seems likely to continue constant, with the Democrats outnumbering Republicans about 5 to 3. There does seem to be a movement away from identifying with either party in favor of self-identification as independents for an increasingly large number of Americans, but previous election studies have shown that these individuals are far less likely to participate in elections than those who identify with a party.

TYPES OF PRESIDENTIAL ELECTIONS

There is a widely used classification scheme for presidential elections, with several variants, that is used to put any given election in its proper long-term context. The most interesting variant of the classification is summarized in Figure 4–2. The figure describes presidential elections on the basis of whether the majority party in terms of party identification of the electorate wins or loses and whether the nature of its support (electoral cleavage) remains the same or changes. Thus, a *maintaining election* is one in which the majority party wins and the nature of support for the two parties remains roughly the same. A *deviating election* is one in which the majority

FIGURE 4-2. A Classification of Presidential Elections

	MAJORITY PARTY	
	Victory	Defeat
ELECTORAL CLEAVAGE — Continuity	"Maintaining"	"Deviating"
ELECTORAL CLEAVAGE — Change	"Converting"	"Realigning"

Source: Gerald Pomper, "Classification of Presidential Elections," *Journal of Politics*, Vol. 29 (August, 1967), p. 538.

party loses for some idiosyncratic reasons but the basic nature of the cleavage between the supporters of the two major parties does not change significantly, at least on a permanent basis. A *converting election* is one in which the majority party wins but the nature of the cleavage changes, providing new converts for at least one of the parties and perhaps for both of them. A *realigning election* is one in which the majority party loses both the election and the basis for its majority status, thus producing a new majority party.

Widely acknowledged realigning elections occurred in 1860, when the Democrats lost their majority status to the Republicans, and in 1932 when the Republicans lost their majority status to the Democrats. Eighteen ninety-six is a good example of a converting election. In that election the Republicans won an overwhelming victory that brought a large segment of the northeastern working class into the Republican party. The Republicans had won seven of the preceding nine elections but usually by close margins. In many ways there was no normal majority party in the 1880s, and so the 1896 election also has elements of a realigning election in it. The year of 1928 is another example of a converting election—the majority Republicans won, but the process of converting the northeastern working class to the Democrats began on a large scale.

The two elections of Democrat Woodrow Wilson (1912 and 1916) in the midst of a Republican era and the two elections of Republican Dwight Eisenhower (1952 and 1956) in the midst of a Democratic era are good examples of deviating elections. Maintaining elections are, of course, the most common, and the elections of Republicans in 1900, 1904, 1908, 1920, 1924 and the elections of Democrats in 1936, 1940, 1944, 1948, and 1960 all fall in this category.

There is, probably inevitably, controversy about the most recent elections: 1964, 1968, and 1972. In 1964 the Democratic candidate, Lyndon Johnson, won an overwhelming victory over Republican Barry Goldwater. At first glance it would seem that this is an obvious case of a maintaining election. But upon closer inspection at least one political scientist, Gerald Pomper, has concluded that 1964 represents a converting election, "retaining the same Democratic party as the majority, but on a new basis of popular support." [16]

In 1968 Republican Richard Nixon won a very narrow victory over Democrat Hubert Humphrey. One analysis, particularly appealing to Democratic partisans, concludes that 1968 represents a deviating election.[17] Another analysis, appealing to Republicans, is that 1968 represents a realigning election that signals the beginning of a new era of Republican dominance.[18]

A less partisan and more rigorous analysis of 1968, again by Pomper, suggests that the Democrats remain as the majority party and that the new voting patterns created in 1964 persisted in 1968, with the obvious difference in the final results:

> The distribution of party identification still heavily favors the Democrats, although there have been major changes within the voting coalition. New voters have been won in suburban areas, among professionals and among blacks, replacing the votes lost among manual workers and Southerners. It should also be underlined that the Democrats nearly won the 1968 election, although short-term influences—urban riots, Vietnam, the Chicago convention, a third party movement, and the Humphrey candidacy—were severely unfavorable.[19]

Pomper's analysis would also seem reasonable when applied to 1972: The Democratic base of support continues to shift but in terms of party identification it remains in a solid majority. It lost the presidency by nominating a candidate that could never shed a "radical" label and who appeared inept at making decisions, but its solid strength was revealed in elections at every other level below the presidential.

[16] Gerald M. Pomper, "Classification of Presidential Elections," *Journal of Politics*, vol. 29 (August, 1967), p. 555.

[17] Richard Scammon and Ben Wattenberg, *The Real Majority* (New York: Coward, McCann, 1970).

[18] Kevin Phillips, *The Emerging Republican Majority* (New Rochelle, N.Y.: Arlington House, 1969).

[19] Gerald M. Pomper, "Control and Influence in American Elections," pp. 222–223.

THE YOUTH VOTE

A new factor that presents some question marks for future trends in voting is the party identification and voting habits of the eighteen- to twenty-one-year-olds who were given the vote in 1971 by the twenty-sixth amendment to the United States Constitution. Some individuals claim that the youth vote will dramatically change the nature of American politics. Others take the more modest view that the new voters might bring about some incremental changes—particularly through local elections in small college towns where the students are allowed to vote in the college town rather than being forced to vote in their parents' town.

It is the latter view that seems most supportable. Several general statements seem accurate:

1. Eighteen-, nineteen-, and twenty-year-olds do not share a common ideology or set of beliefs that set them apart from their older fellow citizens. Diverse opinions on most issues tend to be distributed widely through the population regardless of age. For example, in 1968, media reporting suggested that the young were overwhelmingly "dovish" on Vietnam. The actual distribution of opinion appears in Table 4–5. Not only did "hawks" slightly outnumber "doves" in the under-thirty group, but there were more young "hawks" than older "hawks."

Ideological orientation of the new voters (both newly enfranchised eighteen- to twenty-year-olds and twenty- to thirty-three-year-olds able to vote for the first time in 1972) was tapped in 1971 in a special Gallup poll commissioned by a na-

TABLE 4-5. Vietnam "Hawks" and "Doves" (Self-Identified)

	Under 30	30-49	50 and over
"Hawk"	45%	48%	40%
"Dove"	43%	40%	42%

Source: *Gallup Opinion Index*, report no. 40, (October, 1968) p. 25.

TABLE 4-6. Ideological Orientation of Potential New Voters[a]

Radical Left	Liberal	Middle of the Road	Conservative	Very Conservative
3%	26%	45%	17%	2%

Source: Gallup opinion poll conducted for *Newsweek* magazine. Reported in *Newsweek* (October 25, 1971), p. 49.

a. The sample included 18-23 year olds who would be eligible to vote for the first time in the 1972 national election.

tional news magazine. The ideological distribution, summarized in Table 4–6, leans slightly to the left, but that certainly does not portend a bloc vote. There may be zealots of the "new left," but there are also youthful zealots for George Wallace.

2. Neither party will automatically inherit the eighteen- to twenty-year-old vote. Of these new voters who identify with a party, Democrats outnumber Republicans by a margin greater than two to one, a much stronger preference than that present in the over-twenty-one population. But close to half of the new voters do not identify with either party and prefer to call themselves independents. Both parties will have to work to attract the independent vote. In 1972 eighteen- to twenty-year-olds voted almost as heavily for Nixon as did older voters. Despite party identification, they voted in line with the national trend.

3. The eighteen-, nineteen-, and twenty-year-olds will register less and vote less than older voters. The Gallup estimate was that sixty-five percent of the new voters would be registered to vote in the 1972 election [20] (only twenty-five percent

[20] Gallup poll appearing in *Newsweek* magazine (October 25, 1971) p. 44. This estimate was borne out in Ohio, where only sixty-two percent of those between eighteen and twenty-four were registered. This can be compared to eighty-one percent registration among those twenty-four to forty-four, eighty-five percent in the group forty-five to sixty-four, and eighty-seven percent among those sixty-five and older. *Dayton Daily News* (October 24, 1972).

were registered at the time of the poll); this compares to seventy-five percent of older voters who are registered. Turnout in elections almost always increases with age (up to retirement age). For example, in the 1968 election, fifty-one percent of those twenty-one to twenty-four voted; sixty percent of those twenty-five to twenty-nine voted; seventy-two percent of those thirty to sixty-four voted; and sixty-six percent of those over sixty-five voted. There seems to be no reason to expect that these new voters will not follow this pattern.

IDEOLOGY AND ELECTIONS

There is some evidence that the late 1960s and early 1970s might be one of the exceptional periods in which ideology plays a larger than normal role in American political life. The 1964 election, immersed in rhetoric with a high degree of ideological content, stimulated an unusually high rate of participation on the part of those citizens who were more ideologically oriented than their fellow citizens.[21]

The 1968 election also had a high ideological content, this time stimulated not by major-party candidates who were ideologically oriented but by a minor-party candidate (George Wallace) and a cluster of divisive issues.

One interpretation of the 1968 election, for example, suggests that it had a very strong ideological focus and that it may presage more ideologically oriented voting on the part of the American electorate.[22] Another interpretation along the same lines argues that ideology (particularly clustered around something called the "social issue"—a melange of questions involving race, the generation gap, crime, and changing standards of morality) played a very large role in explaining the outcome of the 1968 presidential contest and some 1969 mayoral contests.[23]

---

[21] John C. Pierce, "Party Identification and the Changing Role of Ideology in American Politics," *Midwest Journal of Political Science*, vol. 14 (February, 1970), pp. 25–42.

[22] Herbert F. Weisberg and Jerrold D. Rusk, "Dimensions of Candidate Evaluation," *American Political Science Review*, vol. 64 (December, 1970), pp. 1167–1185.

[23] Richard M. Scammon and Ben J. Wattenberg, *op. cit.*

In this interpretation, however, a political party that succumbs to the temptation to become consistently and overtly ideological itself will not win elections. The authors argue that the bulk of American opinion is still in the middle of the ideological spectrum and that the party that most effectively captures the center will be most likely to win elections. The results of the 1972 presidential election seems to confirm their position. Rightly or wrongly, the electorate seemed to identify George McGovern as a radical or extremist, and they rejected him as resoundingly as they had rejected Barry Goldwater in 1964.

Other recent studies also suggest that specific issues have taken on such importance and divisive potential that they might create some serious long-term ideological gulfs in the populace that correspond with either racial or class characteristics. For example, one study found that in voting on local referenda involving the Vietnam war, working-class voters tended to be more opposed to the war than middle-class and upper-class voters.[24] An even more serious threat is posed by issues that divide blacks and whites. After analyzing opinion data collected in Detroit following the 1967 riots in that city, two scholars reached the following unsettling conclusion:

> Emerging from our analysis are the outlines of an ominous confrontation between the races. The growing sense of solidarity and racial identification among blacks is being matched by rising, increasingly bitter resentment among elements of the white community. More often than in past decades, the anger and resentment of both sides is being translated from generalized racial hostility into focused political demands for specific programs or policies from agencies of both local and national government.[25]

[24] Harlan Hahn, "Correlates of Public Sentiments about War: Local Referenda on the Vietnam Issue," *American Political Science Review*, vol. 64 (December, 1970), pp. 1186–1198. This possible class division is, of course, softened because the most vocal leaders of the antiwar movement are from the middle and upper classes.

[25] Joel D. Aberbach and Jack L. Walker, "Political Trust and Racial Ideology," *American Political Science Review*, vol. 64 (December, 1970), p. 1215.

CHAPTER 5

Interest Groups

The term *lobbyist* evokes a caricature of a shady, overfed person with currency sprouting from various folds and creases of his apparel. *Interest group* calls to mind a selfish group of men bent on subjugating the national interest and welfare to their own gain. Many lobbyists work for interest groups and the combination is pictured, in the mythology of American government, as powerful and controlling. Legislators, bureaucrats, and even judges are regarded as pawns to be moved at will by these powerful men and the interests they represent.

This picture of the relations between political officials and lobbyists for interest groups grew largely out of some events involving members of Congress in the nineteenth century, when the caricature came close to reality. On a few occasions, such as the Crédit Mobilier affair in the 1870s, members clearly were bribed—in that case, by liberal dispensations of railroad stock. Apparently, congressional approval of the purchase of Alaska in 1867 was secured by liberal dispensations of lobbyists' cash to members of Congress.

Today an occasional attempt at bribery of a senator or representative will come to light. Lavish use of tangible resources to gain the good will and cooperation of an elected legislator is still attempted—as the recent cases of Senator Dodd and Congressman Dowdy sadly show. However, the "old style" lobbying is probably much more prevalent in state legislatures than in Congress.

For the most part, the myth of bribery and all-powerful interest groups and lobbyists has little basis in reality. Most interest groups pursue legitimate interests, most lobbyists are honorable men pursuing a legitimate and honorable trade, and most federal legislators, bureaucrats, and judges are in a position to control the access that lobbyists and interest groups have to them. They can make use of lobbyists on many occasions and do receive valuable informational services from them.

In many ways lobbying is a necessary and useful part of a representative system. It is an adjunct to the party system. The parties primarily elect officials and only secondarily convey opinions of the electorate on policy questions. Lobbies are in business to convey additional policy opinions—at least on the part of the interested parties.

That the interested parties should have a forum for expressing their opinions is clear. That they need some access to the legislative process also seems clear. The danger in lobbying comes when one interest attains a virtual monopoly on the attention of a crucial decision point (a powerful chairman or subcommittee or bureau chief in Congress or the executive branch). Then the competing interests are not considered. There is no balancing of interests but a biasing of decisions in favor of the one interest that is visible and is heard and has exclusive or almost exclusive access. But if access is kept open for competing lobbies (the NAM *and* the AFL–CIO, not just one of them; the Farmers Union *and* the Farm Bureau, not just one of them), then the likelihood of a more balanced judgment by the committee or subcommittee is probably increased, although there are certainly interests that will not be represented at all.

In addition to providing a channel of communication for at least interested individuals and groups in the population, lobbyists can also be useful to legislators and bureaucrats by providing technical information that may not be easily available from other sources. Thus, from the officials' point of view, lobbyists can become potentially valuable sources of that ever-scarce commodity: reliable and timely information.

That the myth of all-powerful lobbyists is not accurate does not imply that interest groups have no impact on public policy. Their impact on the most highly visible parts of federal government activity—the passage or defeat of a major new authorizing statute, for example—is typically not great. Where interest groups can have a large impact is on the less visible, more routine matters of seemingly minor amendments in Congress and seemingly minor administrative adjustments. And because most of the work of the government is of the routine nature, largely invisible and seemingly minor, interest groups and lobbyists do have a large impact on the direction of policy, particularly policy administration. When minor decisions are disaggregated, the impact of lobbyists may seem inconsequential. When those decisions are aggregated, however, the lobbyists' importance grows.

Types of Interest Groups and Lobbyists

There are many different types of interest groups—ranging from large and well-financed to miniscule and impoverished. There are also many types of lobbyists—ranging from full-time professionals to part-time amateurs.

A wide variety of organizations are included under the rubric *interest group*. The large national associations (composed of both individual and organizational members) come to mind first—groups such as the National Association of Manufacturers, the U.S. Chamber of Commerce, and the American Federation of Labor-Congress of Industrial Organizations. There are also a number of industries that have their own national group that is likely to engage in lobbying activities. These groups include, for example, the American Petroleum Institute, the Manufacturing Chemists Association, and the National Coal Association. Some individual corporations may, in some sense, constitute interest groups by themselves. When Boeing and Convair (General Dynamics) were disputing the award of the TFX fighter-plane contract, they were, because of their size and importance, acting as groups and not relying on some other group to represent their interests.

However, groups do not represent only the producer interests of the economy (considering organized labor as a producer, in this instance). There are also groups that represent other units of government: the National Association of Counties, The National League of Cities, and the U.S. Conference of Mayors, for example. Some national groups represent professions and act as interest groups when they become involved in the legislative or administrative process. The American Medical Association and American Bar Association fall in this category. Some professional or semiprofessional groups specifically represent employees of other governmental units. For example, there is a National Association of State Aviation Officials, a National Association of Public Health Officials, and an Airport Operators Council (most airports are owned by a municipality).

Table 5–1 shows the number of different types of organizations registered with the clerk of the House to lobby in Congress during 1970 (in reality from the end of the first session of the Ninety-first Congress to the end of the second session of the Ninety-first Congress). This breakdown of groups indicates both variety and a predominance of business interests at work in lobbying.

The largest interest groups maintain large Washington offices with a number of full-time lobbyists. Smaller groups may maintain a minimal Washington office. A staff of one professional lobbyist, one secretary, and a mimeograph machine is typical of a number of operations. Some groups and companies prefer not to maintain an office of their own but, instead, hire the ubiquitous Washington lawyer to represent their interests. One of this breed of lobbyist may have a number of clients whose interests literally range from soup to nuts.

A number of individuals serving as full-time lobbyists for an association, corporation, or union are retired military offi-

TABLE 5-1. Numbers of Lobbying Organizations Registered with Congress, 1970

Interest Groups	Number of Registrations
Business Groups	223
Citizens Groups	96
Employee and Labor Groups	18
Farm Groups	6
Foreign Groups	8
Foundations	3
Individuals	5
Military and Veteran Groups	3
Professional Groups	11
Total	373

Source: *Congressional Quarterly Almanac* (1970), p. 1208.

cers. Another large contingent are exemployees of the bureaucracy or personal or committee staffs in Congress. Perhaps the most prized catch for an interest group is an ex-senator or ex-representative. These men are particularly valuable because they already know their way around Capitol Hill and have warm personal relationships with a number of the sitting members they are trying to influence. They probably also have a number of potentially useful contacts in the executive branch. Not surprisingly, there are few of this type of lobbyist—only nine former members of Congress or their law firms registered to lobby in 1970. There are more of the retired public officials in action as lobbyists—sixty-six were listed as registered to lobby during the second session of the Ninety-first Congress.[1]

Targets and Techniques of Lobbying

Lobbyists work in all three branches of the government, but the techniques used in each branch vary. Lobbying is directed at members of the House and Senate, bureaucrats and officials

[1] *Congressional Quarterly Almanac* (1970), p. 1208–1213.

within the executive branch, and at judges, and sometimes at the staffs of these individuals. In general lobbying can be depicted as a trade-off process: The lobbyist may have information, often exclusive information, that an official wants and needs, or he may have the potential political weight of voters or campaign contributors. The official, on the other hand, has the power to influence legislation or administration that the lobbyist desires to affect in a particular way.

LOBBYING IN CONGRESS

Congressional lobbying has tended to receive the most attention because of Congress' visibility as an organ of government to which citizens most often petition for redress of grievances and because of the visibility of the lobbying activities themselves in Congress, compared to other branches.

Legislation regulating lobbying activities within Congress has been minimal (partly out of fear of restricting the First Amendment freedoms of free speech and petition in which all lobbying activity is grounded). In 1909 a statute was enacted making it illegal to offer a bribe to a member of Congress and also making it illegal for a member to accept such an offer. The spending of interest groups for political campaigns has been restricted by legislation, since providing or withholding electoral support by a group is an effective way to influence congressmen. The first major legislation dealing with spending, the Federal Corrupt Practices Act of 1925, forbade corporations from making contributions to federal elections. This prohibition was extended to unions in the 1947 Taft-Hartley Act. Restricting spending was also one of the aims of the 1940 Hatch Act, which limited to $5000 the amount that any individual or group could contribute to a federal election campaign in a given calendar year. The effectiveness of these pieces of legislation in actually controlling the impact of interest group spending has been limited because of loopholes within the laws and uncertainty about the application and constitutionality of some of the provisions. As a result, the potential ability of interest groups to influence congressmen's stands on legislation by electoral support or opposition has remained fairly strong.

The only legislation that aims at lobbyist registration was passed by Congress in 1946 (the Federal Regulation of Lobbying Act, passed as Title III of the Legislative Reorganization Act of 1946), although there had been sporadic efforts in the House and Senate in earlier years to pass such legislation. The 1946 act did not restrict the activities of lobbyists, but it did require them (or at least those who were receiving pay for the specific purpose of influencing congressional legislation) to register with the clerk of the House or the secretary of the Senate. Quarterly spending reports were also required of some organizations. The theory behind this law was that by making public the funding sources and legislative interest of lobbyists, congressmen would be better able to evaluate the views of lobbyists with whom they came into contact. Court interpretations, while upholding the constitutionality of the law, have weakened its effectiveness by creating loopholes that permit many groups to avoid registering and filing spending reports.

TABLE 5-2. Interest-Group Registration since 1946

Year	Registrations	Year	Registrations
1946[a]	222	1962	375
1947	731	1963	384
1948	447	Jan. 1, 1964 -	
1949	599	Oct. 3, 1964	255
1950	430	Oct. 4, 1964 -	
1951	342	Oct. 23, 1965	450
1952	204	Oct. 24, 1965 -	
1953	296	Oct. 22, 1966	332
1954	413	Oct. 23, 1966 -	
1955	383	Dec. 15, 1967	449
1956	347	Dec. 16, 1967 -	
1957	392	Oct. 14, 1968	259
1958	337	Oct. 15, 1968 -	
1959	393	Dec. 23, 1969	647
1960	236	Dec. 24, 1969 -	
1961	365	Jan. 3, 1971	373
	Total		9,661

Source: *Congressional Quarterly Almanac* (1970), p. 1208.

[a]last four months only.

Tables 5–2 and 5–3 show the total number of registrations and the spending totals reported since 1946. The number of registrations includes some duplicate registrations, since the law does not require an organization to renew its registration annually. Thus, some groups may register only once, and others may register every year. The spending reported is probably a fraction of actual spending.

Lobbyists use a number of specific techniques in their effort to influence legislative results in Congress. In one technique,

TABLE 5-3. Interest-Group Spending since 1946[a]

Year	Reported Spending ($)
1946[b]	2,297,281
1947	5,191,856
1948	6,763,480
1949	7,969,710
1950	10,303,204
1951	8,771,097
1952	4,823,981
1953	4,445,841
1954	4,286,158
1955	4,365,843
1956	3,957,120
1957	3,818,177
1958	4,132,719
1959	4,281,468
1960	3,854,374
1961	3,986,095
1962	4,211,304
1963	4,223,605
1964	4,223,277
1965	5,484,413
1966	4,656,872
1967	4,751,145
1968	4,298,387
1969	5,420,125
1970	5,841,578

Source: *Congressional Quarterly Weekly Report* (August 6, 1971, p.1680.

a. Court challenges which narrowed the reach of the Federal Regulation of Lobbying Act resulted in a sharp decline in reporting from 1950 on. Varied reporting practices make comparisons uncertain.

b. Reflects figures from August to end of year.

lobbyists appear as witnesses at formal hearings conducted by the various committees and subcommittees of both houses. Typically, they prepare their testimony beforehand and reproduce it in sufficient quantities to pass out to all members of the committee. Occasionally they will distribute it to all members of the House or Senate. At the hearings they read their statement or a synopsis of it. Then they answer whatever questions the committee members may have. If they are particularly close to a member of the committee, they discuss with him before the hearings a line of questioning that will best make the points to support the case in which they are jointly interested.

A second technique is that of personal contact by the lobbyist with the member, usually in his office but perhaps over lunch or a drink. Here, the lobbyist simply tries to argue his case as forcefully as he can. Most lobbyists regard this form of contact as an important technique.

A variation on this technique is the personal contact between the lobbyist and a staff member for a senator or representative or committee in either house. Often the staff-lobbyist relationship becomes more personal and warmer than the member-lobbyist relationship. Lobbyists are aware that staff members often possess partial independence. They cultivate staff members' friendship and support in order to draw on their assistance when necessary.

Naturally, if time is short or if personal rapport has been established, a lobbyist may approach a member of Congress or a staff member by telephone rather than in person.

Sometimes the lobbyist will try to stimulate personal visits or phone calls from other persons he thinks may have some influence on the member of Congress. Thus, if he can convince another senator or representative to "lobby" the member in which he is interested, he may magnify his impact. Or if he stimulates a visit from an important bureaucrat or an important constituent, he is increasing his chances of selling his suggestions to the member.

Another major technique, or rather set of techniques, involves the use of the mail. Lobbyists will often ask a number of the persons for whom they work to write personally to all or selected senators or representatives. They may ask for only a few such letters—from the president of an association or corporation or union, for example, or from the top few officers. Sometimes they try to stimulate a broader mail campaign. In some cases, if a given organization is particularly strong in specific districts, it may try to impress the representatives of those districts by having thousands of letters sent supporting or opposing some specific piece of legislation. An avalanche of mail on a particular issue can impress a legislator a great deal, but if all the letters literally look alike (as is frequently the case when the sponsoring organization provides the forms for mailing), their importance is heavily discounted. A recent example of an effective mail campaign involved the National Rifle Association's efforts to prevent meaningful gun-control legislation. In this case the NRA struck a responsive chord in a large segment of the public, and tons of mail descended on Congress.

Lobbyists may also expend some energies in the districts of members whom they wish to influence. Through gaining the ear of an influential publisher or campaign contributor, they may speak more loudly and forcefully to a member of the House or Senate than by going directly to him. Occasionally, they will mount a more massive effort in the district of a member or members of Congress, trying to persuade a sizable chunk of the public there to aid them in asking a member for specific kind of behavior.

Lobbyists may approach a member of either house as an individual with one vote on the floor, and they may ask for that vote for or against a bill or, often more important, for or against an amendment in which they are particularly interested. Or lobbyists may approach an individual senator or representative because he sits on a committee or subcommittee that is handling a bill in which they are interested. Here they are not asking him to commit himself publicly but instead to aid them in the usual anonymity of the committee room. This anonymity facilitates cooperation between lobbyists and members.

The support or nonsupport that lobbying organizations can give to elected officials as they seek reelection is another important technique. This support is most often in the form of contributions to campaigns, but it also includes endorsements and position papers.

The contribution of interest groups to campaign expenses is critical, especially given the enormous cost of campaigns in the United States.[2] *Congressional Quarterly* estimated as long ago as 1962 that all congressional campaigns that year cost 100 million dollars. In 1968 the Citizens' Research Foundation estimated that all campaigns—presidential, congressional, and local—cost 300 million dollars. In 1970 alone seventeen labor committees spent about three and one-half million dollars, five business and professional committees spent one and one-half million, eleven peace committees spent about half a million dollars, and so did four agricultural committees. Business executives also spent a great deal more as individuals.

This is not to imply that private interests buy the loyalty of candidates by contributing heavily to their election campaigns. Nevertheless, the danger is certainly present that an official who probably could not have won without the financial backing of some specific group will go out of his way to help that group if and when their interests are at stake in some public decision.

LOBBYING IN THE EXECUTIVE BRANCH

Members of the executive branch tend to welcome lobbying as a source of information and, more important, as a source of potential support both with other agencies in the executive branch (particularly the Office of Management and Budget) and in Congress. An agency (typically a bureau) that generates a program idea needs support for that idea in the budget office of its department, in the office of the departmental secretary, and in the Office of Management and Budget. Sometimes, gain-

---

[2] On Campaign financing and spending see Herbert E. Alexander, *Money in Politics* (Washington, D.C.: Public Affairs Press, 1972) and *Congressional Quarterly's Guide to the Congress of the United States* (Washington, D.C.: Congressional Quarterly, 1971), pp. 471–498.

ing support within the bureaucracy is a more difficult task than obtaining it on Capitol Hill. Thus, allies are welcome at an early point in the development of an idea that requires approval of various administrative units or Congress or both.

As group representatives seek to have influence on what goes on in the executive branch, they use a number of specific techniques:

First, they seek to influence the appointment of key personnel in the executive branch. For example, late in the Johnson administration, when the position of Undersecretary of Labor became vacant, the AFL–CIO was in a position to wield a virtual veto over the president's selection to fill the job.

Second, groups will sometimes provide strong support (in terms of selective information and favorable propagandizing) for a program about which they do not care a great deal in order to build up credit that can be drawn on later. In this way groups generate executive-branch support for some program about which the groups do care a great deal.

Third, some interest groups are in the position of having representatives actually become members of the formal decision-making apparatus. For example, until the mid-1950s the Farm Bureau Federation (an interest group) and the Extension Service of the U.S. Department of Agriculture were closely interlocked. There was even a sharing of expenses in supporting county agricultural agents. In a number of agriculture programs there are various committees of farmers and grazers, the membership of which may be dominated by persons allied with specific groups on the state or local level.

Fourth, the ideas for policy statements are sometimes first generated in task forces within the executive branch. The membership of these task forces come from a number of agencies. Typically, various interest groups will seek to gain access to these task forces in order to help shape proposals or at least have their points of view heard at an early stage. Only the more skilled lobbyists actually intrude very significantly at this stage, however.

Fifth, the more knowledgeable lobbyists maintain close personal contacts with a number of key officials in the bureaucracy just for purposes of constantly trading information and views. In this way they become part of the reference group used by bureaucrats when the occasion for a decision affecting their interests arises.

Sixth, on a few occasions interest-group representatives may actually serve temporarily as quasi-staff members for an executive agency, or at least do a large amount of work for the agency. The service they provide is extra help when the agency finds itself shorthanded. In this capacity they can generate considerable information for use by the agency in developing its policy statements and actions. Naturally, the benefit for the interest group is that the information can be developed and presented in such a way as to favor the position espoused by the group.

LOBBYING IN THE JUDICIARY

The federal judiciary is often assumed to be impervious to lobbying efforts. It is certainly true that lobbying as it is carried out in Congress and in the executive branch is not practiced in the judicial branch. This does not mean, however, that interest groups do not try to make an impact on judicial decisions; rather it means that they do so more subtly. Several techniques are used:

First, interest groups become involved in attempting to influence the selection of federal judges for the Supreme Court, the courts of appeals, and the district courts. For example, pro-civil-rights groups lobbied vigorously in the Senate to defeat the nominations of Harold Carswell and Clement Haynesworth for vacancies on the Supreme Court early in the Nixon administration. Their efforts, coupled with the efforts of many others, were successful.

Second, interest groups can file *amicus curiae* (friend of the court) briefs in cases affecting their interests but in which they are not directly involved as litigants. This simply means that the lawyers for a group can argue a position favorable to their interests or views on public policy in a legal document (a brief) that is filed with the other papers in the case and considered by the judges. Thus, for example, the American Jewish

Congress has often filed briefs in cases involving church-state relations. The CIO filed a brief in the case involving the seizure of the steel mills by President Truman in 1952.

Third, interest groups will sometimes sponsor test cases of specific laws by providing high-powered legal services for the individual or individuals protesting the laws. The cases that were decided in 1954 under the rubric of *Brown* v. *Board of Education*, in which the Supreme Court decided that separate public educational facilities for different races violated the Constitution of the United States, were sponsored by the National Association for the Advancement of Colored People.

Fourth, occasionally judges will become the targets of letter-writing campaigns. State, county, and municipal judges are more often targets than are federal judges, however. A more indirect attempt to influence the climate of opinion in the judicial community is sometimes made when lawyers, writing for the interests of groups they represent, argue a certain position in articles and try to get them published in law reviews or bar-association journals—publications that judges read.

The Bias, Effectiveness, and Power of Lobbying and Interest Groups

The interest-representation system (like the rest of the political system) is weighted in favor of the more affluent in society, but it does not exclude the rest of society entirely. Special interests are interests shared by only a relatively small part of the political community. By definition they exclude a wide range of interests and are usually antipathetic to some other special interests. Typically, these special interests are pursued by organized groups. The phenomenon of organized groups pursuing special or private interests is what E. E. Schattschneider, a leading student of interest groups, has called "the pressure system." [3]

[3] E. E. Schattschneider, *The Semisovereign People* (New York: Holt, Rinehart, & Winston, 1960).

101

The Environment for Government Activity

The pressure system is a very small subsystem in the total political system, and it has a predominantly business character. Schattschneider's discussion of the pressure system is a classic and deserves substantial quotation:

> Broadly, the pressure system has an upper-class bias. There is overwhelming evidence that participation in voluntary organizations is related to upper social and economic status; the rate of participation is much higher in the upper strata than it is elsewhere. . . .
>
> The bias of the system is shown by the fact that *even nonbusiness organizations reflect an upper-class tendency.* . . . The obverse side of the coin is that large areas of the population appear to be wholly outside of the system of private organization. . . .
>
> There is a great wealth of data supporting the proposition that participation in private associations exhibits a class bias.
>
> The class bias of associational activity gives meaning to the limited scope of the pressure system, because *scope and bias are aspects of the same tendency.* The data raise a serious question about the validity of the proposition that special-interest groups are a universal form of political organization reflecting *all* interests. As a matter of fact, to suppose that everyone participates in pressure-group activity and that all interests get themselves organized in the pressure system is to destroy the meaning of this form of politics. The pressure system makes sense only as the political instrument of a segment of the community. It gets results by being selective and biased; *if everybody got into the act the unique advantages of this form of organization would be destroyed, for it is possible that if all interests could be mobilized the result would be a stalemate.*
>
> Special-interest organizations are most easily formed when they deal with small numbers of individuals who are acutely aware of their exclusive interests. To describe the conditions of pressure-group organization in this way is, however, to say that it is primarily a business phenomenon. Aside from a few very large organizations (the churches, organized labor, farm organizations, and veterans' organizations) the residue is a small segment of the population. *Pressure politics is essentially the politics of small groups.*
>
> The vice of the groupist theory is that it conceals the most significant aspects of the system. The flaw in the pluralist heaven is that the heavenly chorus sings with a strong upper-

class accent. Probably about 90 per cent of the people cannot get into the pressure system.

The notion that the pressure system is automatically representative of the whole community is a myth fostered by the universalizing tendency of modern group theories. *Pressure politics is a selective process* ill designed to serve diffuse interests. The system is skewed, loaded and unbalanced in favor of a fraction of a minority.

On the other hand, pressure tactics are not remarkably successful in mobilizing general interests. When pressure-group organizations attempt to represent the interests of large numbers of people, they are usually able to reach only a small segment of their constituencies. Only a chemical trace of the fifteen million Negroes in the United States belong to the National Association for the Advancement of Colored People. Only one five-hundredths of 1 per cent of American women belong to the League of Women Voters, only one sixteenth-hundredths of 1 per cent of the consumers belong to the National Consumers' League, and only 6 per cent of American automobile drivers belong to the American Automobile Association, while about 15 per cent of the veterans belong to the American Legion.

The competing claims of pressure groups and political parties for the loyalty of the American public revolve about the difference between the results likely to be achieved by small-scale and large-scale political organization. Inevitably, the outcome of pressure politics and party politics will be vastly different.[4]

The effectiveness of interest groups is strongly affected by their public visibility. On routine issues that are not highly visible to a wide public, interest groups often entrench themselves as part of the policy-making system. On issues that are highly visible to a wide public, interest groups are often less effective.

An important indicator of the relative effectiveness of different types of lobbies is the amount of money that is spent by various groups. Tables 5–4 and 5–5 indicate the reported level of interest group spending during the Ninety-first Congress, second session (1970), both by aggregate group types and by the twenty-five interest groups spending the most in lobbying.

[4] *Ibid.*, pp. 32–36.

TABLE 5-4. Spending by Interest Groups, 1970

Category	Amount Reported ($)
Business	1,901,031
Citizen	1,064,600
Employee and Labor	1,035,815
Farm	600,946
Foreign	32,404
Individual and Firm	42,821
Military and Veteran	569,035
Professional	565,413
Miscellaneous	29,469
Total	5,841,534

Source: *Congressional Quarterly Weekly Report* (August 6, 1971), p.1682.

Note that these figures do not include spending on campaigns, which is considerably greater than spending on lobbying itself. These figures show the predominance of business, labor, and citizens groups in spending.

There is a widely accepted myth about the effectiveness of lobbies—namely that they are powerful, well-financed, well-staffed, efficient, and generally in control of the legislative process and perhaps the bureaucratic process on all questions of public policy. The myth is some distance from reality, however.

Occasionally, perhaps once in a decade, a titanic struggle over a question of public policy will occur that will seem to validate the myth. Thus, the fights like that over the "death sentence" in the utility holding companies legislation in 1935 or that over labor legislation (Landrum-Griffin) in 1959 are magnified by the press so that they seem to be evidence for the general power of lobbies. Two things are wrong with this view. First, such highly visible struggles occur rarely. Second, even in them only *one* set of interest groups and lobbyists emerged victorious. If lobbyists are assumed to be in control of the policy process, at the very least one has to ask: which lobbyists? By definition, if there is competition, not all lobbyists can be in control when their interests conflict. Thus, in the

TABLE 5-5. Twenty-five Top Spenders in 1970

Organization	Dollars Spent
Veterans of World War I, U.S.A. Inc.	341,244
National Association of Letter Carriers (AFL-CIO)	277,125
United Federation of Postal Clerks (AFL-CIO)	228,325
Council for a Livable World	214,626
AFL-CIO (National Headquarters)	197,493
American Farm Bureau Federation	163,553
American Hospital Association	153,241
National Association of Home Builders of the United States	151,605
United States Savings & Loan League	149,794
Citizens Committee for Postal Reform Inc.	138,545
Record Industry Association of America	123,286
Disabled American Veterans	117,134
National Committee for the Recording Arts	99,886
Livestock Producers Committee	96,945
American Medical Association	96,064
National Association of Postal Supervisors	94,661
National Council of Farmer Cooperatives	94,307
National Housing Conference Inc.	92,549
Farmers Educational and Cooperative Union of America	80,738
Common Cause (and Urban Coalition Action Council)	79,347
National Cotton Council of America	79,036
American Legion	78,939
Brotherhood of Railway, Airline & Steamship Clerks, Freight Handlers, Express and Station Employees (AFL-CIO)	75,056
American Trucking Associations Inc.	74,484
International Brotherhood of Teamsters, Chauffeurs, Warehousemen & Helpers of America	72,626

Source: *Congressional Quarterly Weekly Report* (August 6, 1971), p. 1681.

struggle over Landrum-Griffin, it may be accurate in part to say that the Chamber of Commerce and National Association of Manufacturers won, thus proving their power, efficiency, and resourcefulness. But it must also be pointed out, if this interpretation is accepted, that organized labor lost. Does this prove the weakness, inefficiency, and lack of resourcefulness on the part of organized labor? Probably not. Nor does the success of the management groups lead logically to the conclusions that some have drawn about universal and insidious power.

In reality, many interest groups much of the time are under-staffed, underfinanced, and often not terribly adept at conducting the defense of their own interests. Lobbyists are capable of making a number of mistakes that most commentators usually overlook. They are, for example, often paralyzed by internal dissension that prevents them from taking a position early enough in a given legislative struggle to have any effect. They may also unnecessarily aggravate members whom they need by publicly questioning their motives or positions rather than approaching them in private.

Lobbyists are also usually content to concentrate on their friends—or at least on individuals they *think* are their friends. Their problems arise when they misidentify friends and enemies. If they identify a potential friend as an enemy and proceed to ignore him in their efforts to achieve their goals, they are throwing away a potential vote before the struggle has even begun. Often they will identify individuals who are genuinely undecided as definitely in the other camp, again overlooking a potential gain.

Most lobbyists perceive their job to be one that involves providing service and reinforcement to the already convinced official who is friendly to their position. Typically, they do not think it is their job to change the minds of hostile individuals.[5] They are unsure about uncommitted persons and usually approach them gingerly.

Of course, the official-lobbyist relationship is two-way. The official does not simply act at the lobbyists' request. Some officials themselves take the initiative in asking lobbyists to visit them. They figure they can disarm a lobbyist by asking him his position and making compromises, perhaps meaningless and perhaps meaningful, that will have the effect of keeping him out of a given battle.

Officials in the executive branch and members of Congress can also use lobbyists to carry their messages to other lobbyists, to influential constituents, to members of either house, and to

[5] Raymond A. Bauer, Ithiel de Sola Pool, and Lewis A. Dexter, *American Business and Public Policy* (New York: Atherton Press, 1963).

important bureaucrats. Lobbyists play an important role as communicators in a complex communications network in which reliable information is at a premium.

What, then, is a balanced judgment about the impact of lobbyists for interest groups? Interest groups have their greatest impact on matters that *directly* affect interests that they clearly represent. If, for example, a bill changes the price supports for tung nuts, and the tung-nut-growers association shows up to support it or oppose it, the subcommittees of the House Agriculture Committee and Senate Agriculture Committee with jurisdiction over the bill are likely to listen carefully to the point of view and arguments of the association. They, after all, represent the men who make their living by growing tung nuts. If there is a rival point of view from a competing association of growers or from a group representing processors, presumably the subcommittees would listen to these views, too. Similarly, the official in the Department of Agriculture charged with administering the tung-nut program would be likely to be responsive to the same association or associations.

But if, on the same bill or administrative decision, the American Farm Bureau Federation were to come in with a strong position opposite to that of the tung-nut-growers association, their views would probably be accorded little weight. Although they represent farmers, they patently do not represent the interests of the tung-nut growers.

And, if for some reason, the AFL-CIO should choose to announce a position on the tung-nut-supports bill or program, their views would have almost no weight. None of their interests are at stake.

In a sense, the major national associations, such as the NAM, the Chamber of Commerce, the Farm Bureau, and the AFL-CIO, dilute their effectiveness because they speak on so many issues. They make general pronouncements on budgetary matters, foreign affairs, and the state of the union. Also, their power is less than it may appear at first glance because they represent a variety of interests, some of which may logically conflict with each other. Two member unions in the AFL-CIO may disagree on the provisions of a given bill. What can the

AFL-CIO do in this case? Usually it would choose to stay quiet and inactive. If two industries in the NAM had a conflict over a bill, the NAM itself might be forced to stay out.

Also, empirical research indicates that most interest groups have more effect on amendments and less visible matters than final passage or defeat of sweeping legislation. Although these amendments are less visible to the public and thus seemingly less important, this may be precisely where the interests of the group are most directly at stake. The danger for the public lies in that close associations of individual lobbyists, members of Congress, staff members, and bureaucrats may decide these less visible, but often important, questions in accord only with the narrow interests of the group and with little attention to the broader concerns of the general public.

A classic example of the power of a lobby on a relatively invisible issue is provided by an administrative decision on milk price supports in 1971.[6] On March 12 the secretary of agriculture announced that the support level would remain unchanged from the previous year. Less than two weeks later, however, he announced that the price-support level would be increased by almost six percent (an increase that represented about 300 million dollars in increased subsidies for 1971). During the interim period the Agriculture Department and White House were lobbied by representatives of the milk industry *and* by the friends of the industry and of dairy farmers in Congress. One large cooperative, representing about ten percent of all of the milk production in the nation, led the attack. The dairy lobbyists even got an hour's audience with the president himself. The only opposition to the increase came from one other milk company that felt it had been subjected to unfair competitive practices by the cooperative that spearheaded the effort to obtain the administrative increase.

In short, the public focus on interest groups is often at the wrong end of the policy process. The focus is on the beginning—the passage of major organic statutes establishing new

[6] Frank Wright, "The Dairy Lobby Buys the Cream of the Congress," *Washington Monthly* (May, 1971), pp. 17-21.

programs—where, most of the time, interest groups are least effective and influential. In reality, however, the most influential interest-group work comes in either obtaining or preventing specific amendments to legislation, specific line items in appropriations statutes, or specific decisions about how to interpret a statute or executive order in the implementation process in the bureaucracy.

The Public and Its Leaders: A Summary View of Linkages

Before concluding this section on the environment for government activity and the linkages between the public and its leaders, it should be noted that neither political parties nor interest groups are monoliths. They are usually composed of factions all struggling with one another for dominance. Thus, the stance of a party or of an interest group (particularly the larger ones) may shift from time to time.

That parties are the object of internal struggle is evident. The Goldwater-Rockefeller-Scranton battle in 1964 in the Republican party and the McGovern-Humphrey-Muskie-Jackson battle in 1972 in the Democratic party were not merely struggles between candidates sharing the same views on public policy. Instead they were struggles between different factions within each of the parties, and each of the principal factions held some views quite at odds with some of the views of the other principal factions.

Interest groups are also prone to internal division and debate and competition for influence, although the struggle in such groups may be more personal than ideological.

Keeping the above qualification in mind, the last four chapters, which have focused on the linkages between the citizenry and their government, can now be summarized. Figure 5–1 summarizes the nature of those linkages from two perspectives: that of the public and that of the officials. In general, it can be seen that there are direct two-way relationships between the public and its leaders and officials. There are also indirect or

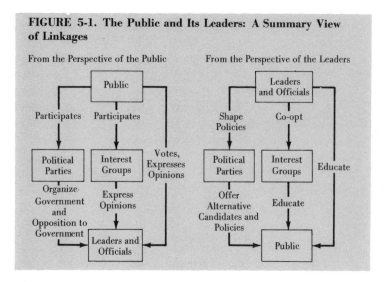

FIGURE 5-1. The Public and Its Leaders: A Summary View of Linkages

mediated relationships that go in both directions, with political parties and interest groups playing crucial mediating roles.

The relationships portrayed neither give complete control of the government and its policies to leaders and officials nor do they allow the public to determine more than the general shape of governmental activity in many areas (although interest groups may be important influences on a variety of specific matters, too). The channels of access are sufficient to allow the government to be called, in a general way, representative. However, the channels can become clogged or can be biased in specific directions. Thus, it is here argued that the representational relationship does not afford perfect representation of policy wishes, but neither does this relationship deny the possibility of genuine, often sustained, representation of such wishes.

PART **3**

The Structure
of
Government

CHAPTER 6

The Presidency

Even though the president is a highly visible individual that everyone in the country with the least interest in politics can identify, the presidency is, in many ways, an elusive office (or set of offices) to understand. Logically it should be easy to grasp what the president does and how he goes about doing it, mainly because the mass media report virtually his every movement. Yet, there are many ambiguities in the office, and there are a number of open questions about it that any incumbent faces and that, therefore, any citizen wishing to ponder the presidency also faces.

Presidential Roles

The president plays a number of roles and is sometimes cross-pressured by role conflicts. One major source of confusion for the analyst and perhaps for the president is that he is

113

called on to play a number of different roles simultaneously. Some of the expectations attached to one role will conflict with the expectations attached to another role. Thus, in any given situation, a president may well be torn in terms of the proper course of behavior, because he perceives the conflicting demands and is faced with the necessity of choosing between them.

At the same time, however, the role conflicts facing a president also help give him a good deal of flexibility as he faces what must surely be one of the world's most demanding jobs. That is, a clever president, who perceives the different demands, can play one off against the other in a given situation and perhaps reverse the process in a subsequent situation. But the critical fact is that he has some degree of choice in the matter, at least a good deal of the time. Even though surrounded by an enormous array of institutions and individuals constantly petitioning him for a variety of actions and favors, the president can, at least in those matters about which he cares most, retain a good deal of autonomy.

A number of analysts have listed a variety of roles for the president.[1] There are three major roles that seem to occupy a good deal of any president's time.

First, the president must play a role as head of state. In this role he is the ceremonial head of the nation and a symbol of national unity, will, and purpose. Some of the demands of this role include a stress on a president above politics and above divisive controversy.

Second, the president plays a role as head of government. In this role his job is to make the government work. Naturally, it is unrealistic to expect any one man, even armed with the formal powers of the office, to control very much of the government. However, the public and the press tend to hold the president responsible for whatever the government does or does not produce during his administration. Thus, he has to spend a good deal of his energy trying to motivate other parts of the government to do something resembling his bidding—or

[1] See, for example, Clinton Rossiter, *The American Presidency* (New York: Harcourt Brace and Jovanovich, 1956) for one well-known listing of ten roles.

at least he has to help create the illusion that other parts of the government are doing something in response to his requests and priorities. He must contend with a variety of governmental personnel—his own appointees (who, once appointed, tend to transfer their loyalty to the specific institution with which they have become associated rather than maintaining personal loyalty to the president); with civil servants who staff most of the jobs in the bureaucracy, including many of the policy-making jobs, and who are secure in their jobs because of civil-service laws and regulations; and with members of the House and Senate, who have their own electoral bases, independent of the president's.

The president functioning to cajole the government into action (or, occasionally, into inaction) has been the subject of considerable attention. Thomas Cronin's description is useful:

> Contemporary policy studies suggest that the more we learn about presidential policy performance, the more it appears that presidents (in both domestic and foreign policy) only rarely accomplish policy "outcomes" that can be credited as distinct personal achievements. More realistically, the presidency serves as a broker for a few party priorities and as a strategically situated and important participant among vast numbers of policy entrepreneurs and policy-bearing bureaucrats. More often than not a president's personal policy views are essentially moderate and only vaguely refined. When in office, however, he finds himself constantly surrounded by people who have "high-energy" interest and investments in specific policy outcomes.[2]

Richard Neustadt has also written insightfully of the president and has concluded that the basic power the president has is the power to persuade. "The essence of a president's persuasive task with congressmen and everybody else, *is to induce them to believe that what he wants of them is what their own appraisal of their own responsibilities requires them to do in their interest, not his.*"[3] The formal powers of command that

[2] Thomas E. Cronin, "Superman, Our Textbook President," *The Washington Monthly*, vol. 2 (October, 1970), p. 54.

[3] Richard E. Neustadt, *Presidential Power*, Signet ed. (New York: New American Library, 1960), p. 53.

the president possesses are rarely usable in their pristine form, and even their effectiveness is limited. Most of the time the president must play the "broker" role as he labors to make the government appear effective in the production and implementation of policy. He must parlay what Neustadt calls his vantage points in government (that is, his critical position as a broker) plus the additional weight he can derive from his reputation for effectiveness within the policy-making community in Washington and his prestige in the nation as a whole so as to maximize his chances for influencing policy statements and actions in directions of his own preference.

Third, the president plays an important role as head of party. Virtually all presidents are vitally interested in the future of their party. Most have been well-known partisan figures for most of their careers before becoming president. Of the twelve presidents elected in this century nine have held elective office at either the senatorial or gubernatorial level (four were, in addition, vice-presidents, and three also had House service prior to Senate service). Of the three who had never been elected to any major post, only one (Dwight Eisenhower) had never held a cabinet position. Both William Howard Taft and Herbert Hoover, although not experienced in electoral politics, had been longtime and quite visibly important cabinet members for presidents of their own party. Thus, in general, it can be asserted that our presidents in this century have been experienced political figures.

Given their partisan pasts, it is not surprising that most presidents are also interested in keeping the presidency under the control of their own party—either through their own reelection or through the election of a successor of the same party. Thus, most presidents weigh the political costs and benefits of a number of their actions, and party activists expect such behavior. The potential for conflict between this role and the head-of-state role is obvious; it can also conflict with the head-of-government role.

When faced with cross-pressures, presidents are forced to decide which role to emphasize, and they make different choices at different times. It should also be noted, of course, that not all situations produce cross-pressures. There are situations in which the values of two or sometimes all three roles can be served simultaneously without making sacrifices.

Several recent examples will serve to illustrate presidents making different choices. When President Lyndon Johnson announced in March of 1968 that he would not seek reelection the following fall, he appears to have been putting his role as head of state ahead of his other two primary roles. After announcing that he was stopping the bombing in much of North Vietnam and discussing the entire situation in Vietnam, he discussed the question of national unity and his own role in it:

> There is division in the American house now. There is divisiveness among us all tonight. And holding the trust that is mine, as President of all the people, I cannot disregard the peril to the progress of the American people and the hope and the prospect of peace for all peoples. . . .
>
> What we won when all of our people united just must not now be lost in suspicion, distrust, selfishness, and politics among any of our people.
>
> Believing this as I do, I have concluded that I should not commit the Presidency to become involved in the partisan divisions that are developing in this political year.
>
> With America's sons in the fields far away, with America's future under challenge right here at home, with our hopes and the world's hopes for peace in the balance every day, I do not believe that I should devote an hour or a day of my time to any personal partisan causes or to any duties other than the awesome duties of this office—the Presidency of your country.
>
> Accordingly, I shall not seek, and I will not accept, the nomination of my Party for another term as your President.[4]

By taking this position Johnson was trying to symbolize national unity. At the same time, however, he was putting his party in a precarious position because he would probably have won reelection had he run. He was also telling the government that he was not going to be president much longer, and so the members of Congress and the bureaucrats who did not agree with his policies anyway had little incentive left to try to please him and his close staff associates.

[4] *Public Papers of the President, Lyndon B. Johnson, 1968–1969.* Vol. 1 (Washington, D.C.: Government Printing Office, 1970), pp. 475–476.

Another example involves both Presidents Kennedy and Johnson. Both of them assiduously courted Senator Everett M. Dirksen, the Republican Minority Leader of the Senate, by consulting regularly with him in settings designed to give him maximum publicity as a statesman without whom no president could manage. They also were both publicly vocal about giving Dirksen major portions of credit for a variety of legislative actions they had requested from Congress. Here, both presidents were judging that such consultation, flattery, and publicity were helpful to them in their role as head of government. Part of their job in that role is to help push specific legislation through Congress. They calculated that wooing Dirksen would help facilitate the passage of more of what they thought the nation needed. At the same time, of course, they were sacrificing part of their role as head of party because they were publicly allocating part of the credit to a national Republican figure, thus withholding that share from the leaders of their own party.

An example in which the head-of-party role reigned supreme involved President Harry Truman. In his speech accepting the Democratic nomination in 1948, he announced that he was going to call the Republican-controlled Congress back into session to make them deliver immediately on the promises contained in their platform. Truman describes the situation in his memoirs:

> I listed in detail the failures of the Republican-controlled Congress and I did not pull any punches. Then, toward the end of the speech, I played my trump card. I announced: . . . "I am going to call Congress back and ask them to pass laws to halt rising prices, to meet the housing crisis—which they (the Republican party) are saying they are for in their platform.
>
> "At the same time, I shall ask them to act upon other needed measures, such as aid to education, which they say they are for; a national health program; civil rights legislation, which they say they are for; . . . extension of the Social Security coverage and increased benefits, which they say they are for. . . .
>
> "Now my friends, if there is any reality behind that Republican platform, we ought to get some action from a short

session of the Eightieth Congress. They can do this job in fifteen days, if they want to do it. . . ."

This announcement of a special session of the Congress electrified the convention to a new pitch of confidence and enthusiasm. I was telling the Democrats that we were calling the bluff of the Republican opposition and that we were going to fight them with everything we had.

Of course I knew that the special session would produce no results in the way of legislation. But I felt justified in calling the Congress back to Washington to prove to the people whether the Republican platform really meant anything or not. Every item of legislation which I called essential to the welfare of the country was included in the Republican platform and needed to be acted upon without delay. Yet I knew they would run out on their platform.[5]

The maneuver worked in that the special session did nothing and Truman made his attack on the Republican-controlled Congress a major feature of his winning campaign that fall. At the same time, of course, he was decidedly not a figure of national unity. But his judgment was that the necessities of re-election demanded that he sacrifice, temporarily, his head-of-state role to his head-of-party role.

Richard Nixon's first three years as president also provide a number of examples of situations in which the president was cross-pressured and made different choices.[6] For example, his initiative in trying to improve relations with the People's Republic of China, dramatized by a personal visit, stressed his role as head of state—symbolizing supposed national unity in seeking to reduce world tensions and produce permanent peace. (It also seems reasonable to speculate that the president was aware of changing public opinion toward China. Data in Table 2–3 in this volume, for example, show a steadily increasing percentage of the population favoring the admission of China to the United Nations, and in 1971, for the first time, those favoring admission were more numerous than those opposing

[5] Harry S. Truman, *Years of Trial and Hope*, Signet ed. (New York: New American Library, 1965), pp. 241–42.

[6] For an account of these three years, see Rowland Evans and Robert D. Novak, *Nixon in the White House: The Frustration of Power* (New York: Random House, 1971).

it.) At the same time, Nixon ran some political risk because conservative members of both parties, long accustomed to hearing and making public denunciations of Red China, resisted accepting the new approach to China. Also, the supersecret handling of the initiative may have offended some leading members of the president's party who had not been consulted about the new policy and who were caught by surprise along with everyone else.

On another front, Nixon's decision in his first term not to assault directly the existence of a large number of domestic programs that had come into existence under the Democratic New Frontier and Great Society represented a decision that put primary weight on his role as head of government. Rather than dismantling programs with the made-by-Democrats label he changed some of their emphases to make them more palatable to Republicans.[7] But he did not propose simply discontinuing them, although some Republicans were eager to do so. Indeed, Nixon heeded the advice of Daniel P. Moynihan, a liberal Democrat he had induced to enter his administration and serve in an important White House position, that continuity would be perceived as less threatening by the bureaucracy and Congress (both dominated by Democrats and those sympathetic to the programs in question) than discontinuity. Thus, in this instance Nixon served the values in his head-of-government role but did not attempt to exploit some possible partisan advantage that might emerge from dismembering Democratic programs and replacing them with Republican programs. At the beginning of his second term in 1973, however, Nixon changed his stance and proposed termination of most Great Society domestic programs and their replacement by revenue-sharing.

In the field of civil rights, Nixon's performance appeared to make the head-of-state and head-of-government roles subservient to the head-of-party role. As part of the so-called southern strategy for winning reelection in 1972 and simultaneously

[7] For examples of four programs (economic development, Job Corps, model cities, and aid to Appalachia) treated this way by Nixon, see Randall B. Ripley, *The Politics of Economic and Human Resource Development* (Indianapolis, Ind.: Bobbs-Merrill, 1972).

building the permanent strength of the Republican party, Nixon wanted to deny any avid administration interest in pushing desegregation. Thus, he and his chief advisors directed the government to go slow in implementing measures aimed at increasing the rate of public school desegregation. The administration disavowed any interest in helping integrate white suburbia. And the president came out against busing to achieve racially balanced schools. These were stances taken presumably to encourage the white, conservative voters of the South to vote for Nixon in 1972 and to regard the Republican party as friendly. But, at the same time, these actions alienated large numbers of government employees in the Departments of Justice and Health, Education, and Welfare. The open revolt of some of these employees made the president, in effect, responsible for complicating rather than simplifying the task of making these two departments of government work. The president also effectively denied himself the chance of trying to forge national unity behind any particular policy on racial questions. Instead, he exacerbated already deep societal divisions.

Presidential Style and Orientation

Presidents have considerable leeway in how they perform the duties of their office; they can choose some features of their basic orientation; other features are more fixed.

From the beginning, the presidency has been both an enormously powerful office and, at the same time, a highly bounded office. A good deal of this contradiction is simply written into the Constitution. One of the leading students of the presidency, Edwin S. Corwin, has written succinctly and persuasively about these contradictions:

> It is an axiom of American history that the Constitution came from the framers "a bundle of compromises." Not so generally recognized is the confirmation which is lent this observation by those clauses of the Constitution most nearly affecting the office and powers of the President. The vague-

ness of the constitutional grants of power to the President has always furnished matter for comment, sometimes favorable, sometimes otherwise, depending on the commentator's bias. "The executive power shall be vested in a President of the United States of America"; "the President shall be Commander-in-Chief of the Army and Navy"; with the advice and consent of the Senate he shall make treaties and appoint to office; he shall have power to "grant pardons for offenses against the United States," he shall "recommend . . . such measures to Congress, as he shall judge necessary and expedient"; and so on and so forth. Yet, in order to exercise any of these powers—in order, indeed, to subsist—he must have money, and can get it only when and if Congress appropriates it. Likewise, he is dependent on Congress for the very agencies through which he must ordinarily exercise his powers, and Congress is the judge as to the necessity and propriety of such agencies. Again, he is bound to "take care that the laws" which Congress enacts are "faithfully executed"—for this purpose all his powers are in servitude; and Congress has the power to investigate his every official act, and can, by a special procedure, if it finds him guilty of "high crimes and misdemeanors," impeach him and throw him out of office. Moreover, by the standard set by the prerogative of the British monarch in 1787, his "executive power" and his power to protect that power were seriously curtailed. The power to "declare war" was vested in Congress; the Senate was made a participant in his diplomatic powers; he was given a veto upon all legislative acts, but this the houses may override by a two-thirds vote.

In short, the Constitution reflects the struggle between two conceptions of executive power: the conception that it ought always to be subordinate to the supreme legislative power, and the conception that it ought to be, within generous limits, autonomous and self-directing; or, in other terms, the idea that the people are *re-presented* in the legislature *versus* the idea that they are *embodied* in the executive. Nor has this struggle ever entirely ceased, although on the whole it is the latter theory which has prospered.[8]

The presidency, then, contains an inbuilt ambiguity that allows every incumbent considerable leeway in the way he performs the duties of office. He can either emphasize the powers

[8] Edwin S. Corwin, "The Presidency in Perspective," *Journal of Politics*, vol. 11 (1949), pp. 7–8.

inherent in the office and seek to maximize them or he can stress the limits on those powers and shrink from certain kinds of action.

A quick review of the history of the presidency suggests that presidents have indeed chosen different paths. The same review also supports the view that an increasing proportion of presidents have moved toward the pole of action and away from the pole of restraint on the spectrum of presidential activity.[9]

In the eighteenth and nineteenth centuries the modal president leaned toward restraint. The exceptions—Washington, Jefferson, Jackson, and Lincoln—were activists. Only during the twenty-eight years (one-fourth of the period between 1789 and 1901) in which these four men were president was the holder of the office consistently aggressive in expanding the powers of the office and pushing against its limits. The other presidents varied but were, at most, aggressive only sporadically (like Polk, for example, in relation to territorial expansion). Some were quite inactive (Fillmore, Pierce, and Buchanan, for example).

In the twentieth century the pattern has changed. Now the modal president leans toward the activist end of the spectrum. Since 1901 the two Roosevelts, Wilson, Truman, Kennedy, Johnson, and, in many ways, Nixon, have all fit that pattern. Only Taft, Harding, Coolidge, Hoover, and Eisenhower can be classified as leaning toward the pole of restraint, and of those only Coolidge really resembles a Fillmore or Pierce. Thus, during the first seventy-two years of this century an activist president has held office two-thirds of the time (the forty-eight years during which the seven activists named above have held office).

The differences between activist presidents and presidents intent on self-restraint are, of course, not black and white. Even the most active and powerful presidents have fortunately refrained from some possible exercises of their power. And even

[9] The terms *restraint* and *action* are used by Edwin Hargrove to suggest two ends of a spectrum. See Edwin Hargrove, *Presidential Leadership* (New York: Macmillan, 1966).

the most passive presidents have occasionally shown some aggressiveness on something about which they cared a great deal.

The question of why the character of the presidency seemed to change so relatively dramatically right around the turn of the century is an interesting one. At least the following factors seem to have been at work:

1. Following the Civil War the federal government had gradually taken a number of new enterprises under its wing and, in the late 1880s and 1890s had put itself into the regulatory endeavor. The first measures and the early enforcement of those measures were somewhat timid by modern standards. But the government nonetheless had become, at least potentially, a more visible and important force in society by extending its jurisdiction into the regulatory arena, an arena marked by hot and widespread political debate throughout society at the same period. Thus, in a sense, if the government was becoming a more potent domestic force, the president also stood to become more important domestically.

2. With the Spanish-American War in 1898 the United States suddenly emerged as a world power. Its resources and population clearly qualified it for major-power status, and now, for the first time in its national history, the nation appeared willing to back its potential act with acts of will—first, pushing over the Spanish in both the Caribbean and the Pacific and then enunciating the Open Door policy for China. Armed conflict or the possibility of armed conflict had always enhanced the importance of the president; once the United States had thrust itself into the middle of world politics, that potential became much more real and seemed to demand a president of greater visibility and activity.

3. To the above contextual factors that probably would have produced the modern presidency at some time can be added the accident of Theodore Roosevelt's personality and the timing of his accession to the presidency because of an assassination. Roosevelt wanted and enjoyed presidential power; he wanted the government to pursue vigorous regulatory policies domestically, and he also wanted the United States to assume what he

considered its rightful place in the world order through being active and sometimes aggressive.

Sidney Hyman, in summarizing the various stances that presidents might take toward their powers, offers a lively and interesting description in which he portrays a "Buchanan concept" of the office at the pole of restraint, a "Lincoln concept" at the pole of action, and a "Cleveland concept" in the middle. His discussion is worth quoting at length:

> Taken in order, the Buchanan concept rejects the idea of a President as the political leader of the nation. He is rather, as President Grant expressed it, "a purely administrative officer." This means that the main function of the President is to be efficient, honest, decorous, pious, and that he should get 100 cents out of every dollar spent. He should not have any vibrant two-way connections with the argumentative political earth of the nation. He should not engage in personalities. He should not make his own political consciousness—if he has any at all—the source of a national political consciousness. He should never make any great demands on the people. As a model of self-abnegation, he should diminish his own size in the eyes of the people.
>
> The very last thing he should do is to view his Presidential oath of office as a reserve source of power that could rally the nation when all other organs of government stall in a crisis. Buchanan, for example, offered the legal opinion in January, 1860, that he had no power to use force against the seceding Southerners. All he or anyone else in the Government could do was to "conciliate them." Come what may, in any movement of his parts, the Buchanan concept limits the President to a tight legal circuit involving the Congress and the Court.
>
> Nor within that tight legal circuit should he be the main source of energy, leading the Congress from above. The political initiative rests always with the Congress. It remains for the President merely to administer the objects and situations defined for him by the Congress. In this general view of things, then, a good President is one who best integrates himself with the Congressional group.
>
> The Lincoln concept of the Presidency begins where the Buchanan concept ends. Political instead of legalistic in emphasis, it is highly articulate, highly argumentative, and it has a keen taste for political battle. Its view of man is nonangelic. It accepts conflict as a natural aspect of life itself. And since

125

it does, it looks upon partisan politics as a creative instrument that can define and, to some extent at least, resolve things in dispute.

Since it is bent on change and innovation, it tries at times to race ahead and, by the measures taken, to produce, instead of await, an event. From this cause, it seems to be super-charged with willfulness. It communicates a will to decide, a will to force the proof that the decision was correct and a will to assume primary responsibility for what was decided. "Send the problem over to me," Roosevelt often used to say to his aides. "My shoulders are big enough to carry it." And Truman said much the same thing with the well-known sign on his desk reading: "The buck stops here."

From all these causes, the Lincoln concept makes the President himself something more than an administrative officer or a civil service reformer or a chief of state or a comptroller of the currency. It makes the President the nation's first legis-lator, the inventor, as well as the executor of policy, the source as well as the summation of the nation's political con-sciousness. In every major crisis, it places the President in the most exposed position of the firing line, like a patriot king leading troops in battle.

"Those who accept great charges," said Jefferson in refer-ence to his own conduct as President, "have a duty to risk themselves on great occasions, when the safety of the nation or some of its very high interests are at stake." And Lincoln repeated after him: " felt that measures, otherwise unconsti-tutional, might become lawful by becoming indispensable to the preservation of the Constitution through the preservation of the nation."

The Lincolnian concept, finally, does not raise the Presi-dent over the Congress or the Court. It accepts the Constitu-tional proposition that each of these must be strong in its own right to do its own work. Each has a duty to preserve its own integrity against invasion by another. None can surrender its organic powers and duties even by a voluntary act.

The Cleveland concept of the Presidency shuttles between the other two. Now it seems to say the Presidential office is chiefly an administrative one; now it seems to say that it is also a political one. Now it talks of leading a march toward brave new horizons; now it draws back from the adventure. Now it seems prepared to follow the lead of the Congress; now it seems disposed to tell the Congress to mind its own business and to keep its nose out of Executive business.

Yet, if there is any distinctive trait about Clevelandism, it is the fact that in this concept of the Presidency the essential Presidential function lies in defensive directions. It lies in the legal (or political) veto, in disengagement, in the negation of what others have put into motion, or in the use of only enough Executive energy to maintain an existing kinetic equilibrium. It was Cleveland, for example, who informed the Congress that, if it declared war on Spain, he could not be counted on to run the war. It was John Adams, almost a century earlier, who said virtually the same thing to his own Federalist party when it demanded a full-scale war against France.[10]

In some ways the Buchanan concept probably belongs to history; no future president is likely ever to be in a position that would allow the inactivity that concept suggests. The institutional presidency provides a good deal of continuity to the office that almost guarantees a certain level of activity. For example, in 1953 when incoming President Eisenhower expressed doubts about the utility of having a presidential legislative program, the Bureau of the Budget, staffed mostly by career people who had served Roosevelt and Truman, quickly persuaded him that not to have such a program would have very bad results for the presidency and for the country. Consequently, in 1954 the Eisenhower administration put together a far-reaching, comprehensive legislative program; no president since has failed to assume that duty as part of his job.[11]

An old debate on presidential power has, in recent years, broken out again, largely as a result of the American involvement in Indo-China. This debate is over whether the president is too powerful and whether he is subverting the intent of the Constitution to make Congress a full partner in the governing process, particularly in the matter of declaring war. Presidents in the last several decades have taken a number of actions to commit the United States to specific courses of international

[10] Sidney Hyman, "What Is the President's True Role?" *New York Times Magazine*, September 7, 1957, p. 17. © by The New York Times Company. Reprinted by permission.
[11] Richard E. Neustadt, "Presidency and Legislation: Planning the President's Legislative Program," *American Political Science Review*, vol. 49 (December, 1955), pp. 980–1021.

action with only minimal or nonexistent congressional involvement. President Roosevelt virtually unilaterally traded Great Britain fifty destroyers for some bases in the Caribbean before the United States became involved in World War II. He also ordered American troops to Iceland to prevent German occupation of that country before the United States was in the war. President Truman sent American troops to Korea without congressional approval. President Eisenhower sent them to Lebanon. And, of course, Presidents Eisenhower, Kennedy, Johnson, and Nixon all conducted the Vietnam War without much reference to Congress, except for a very vaguely worded resolution in 1964.

Some members of both the public and of the House and Senate have responded by demanding a closer congressional scrutiny of the president's war-making power. A variety of attempts has been made to end the war legislatively, usually by denying funds for the operation beyond a certain date. Some hortatory resolutions have also been offered. Although Congress formally repealed the Tonkin Gulf resolution (in early 1971) that repeal had no visible effect. The enactment of the Cooper-Church amendment in 1970 to deny funds for support of U.S. operations in Cambodia had little practical effect because the operation was planned for a short period of time anyway.[12]

The Institutional Presidency

The development of an institutional presidency has provided increasingly large elements of stability and continuity in the performance of presidential tasks. All presidents have, of course, had some staff help. But only in the 1930s did the presidency begin to develop permanent institutional supports for the indi-

---

[12] For a substantial selection from the fascinating debate in the Senate on the Cooper-Church amendment to force the president to withdraw American troops from Cambodia, see Theodore J. Lowi and Randall B. Ripley, eds., *Legislative Politics U.S.A.* 3rd ed. (Boston: Little, Brown, 1973).

vidual holding the office. Beginning with Franklin Roosevelt, all presidents have helped contribute to the growth of the institutional presidency. This includes President Eisenhower, whose administration made some of the major contributions to institutionalization.

As of July 1, 1971, the Executive Office of the President had sixteen parts. These are listed in Table 6–1, along with their date of creation and the size of their staff. It should be noted that the Office of Economic Opportunity is unique in the Executive Office. It has primarily operating responsibilities, although it is supposedly also a coordinating agency. It was the latter that provided the original rationale for locating the agency in the Executive Office. (An additional factor in choosing its bureaucratic location was a jurisdictional battle waged in the executive branch in 1963 and 1964 over the question of its location; putting the agency in the Executive Office of the President was a compromise.) It should also be noted that OEO will go out of existence altogether if President Nixon has his way.

Size of staff suggests that the White House Office and the Office of Management and Budget are the two key staff arms of the presidency, and that in fact is the case. The Office of Emergency Preparedness has a large staff but is not a consistently important part of the presidency. Instead, three less amply staffed units—the Council of Economic Advisers, the National Security Council, and the Domestic Council—round out the most important part of the institutional presidency.

The White House Office is the President's private preserve. His various special assistants—men such as John Ehrlichman, H. R. Haldeman, Robert Finch, and Henry Kissinger for President Nixon and men such as Lawrence O'Brien, Walt Rostow, and McGeorge Bundy for Presidents Kennedy and Johnson—all are part of the White House Office. Basically the staff in this office does whatever the president wants. Practically speaking, the office must focus on policy development (both domestic and foreign), relations with the press and public, and relations with Congress. Beginning with President Eisenhower, the congressional-relations section of the White House Office

129

TABLE 6-1. The Executive Office of the President, 1971

Unit	Date of Creation as Part of Executive Office[a]	Size of Staff Fiscal 1971	Size of Staff Fiscal 1972 (Estimate)
White House Office	1939	533	540
Office of Management and Budget	1939	657	684
Council of Economic Advisors	1946	57	57
National Security Council	1947	70	75
National Aeronautics and Space Council	1958	21	16
Office of Emergency Preparedness	1958	235	223
Office of Science and Technology	1962	50	50
Office of the Special Representative for Trade Negotiations	1963	30	34
Office of Economic Opportunity[b]	1964	2478	2025
Office of Intergovernmental Relations	1969	9	9
Council on Environmental Quality	1969	50	57
Office of Telecommunications Policy	1970	48	65
Domestic Council	1970	52	70
Council on International Economic Policy	1971	c	c
Office of Consumer Affairs	1971	35	50
Special Action Office for Drug Abuse Prevention	1971	—	172

Source: Compiled from data in the *Budget of the United States Government, Fiscal 1973, Appendix* (Washington, D.C.: Government Printing Office, 1971), pp. 986 ff.

a. Or date of creation of the predecessor agency.
b. Basically an operating agency.
c. Legislation authorizing creation and staffing of this unit had not been approved when the budget went to press; hence figures on size of staff were not available.

has developed into a formal staff. The Watergate scandal that rocked the Nixon White House had the immediate effect of decimating the White House staff (including Ehrlichman and Haldeman). It may have the more permanent effect of making White House staff members subject to increased continuing public scrutiny.

The Office of Management and Budget is less personally responsive to the president, but it provides the bulk of the continuity in the institutional presidency. White House staff members come and go with different presidents; turnover is complete and instantaneous when a new man enters office, especially if he is of a different political party than his predecessor. This is true even when a vice-president accedes to the presidency in the middle of the term. When Lyndon Johnson became president following John Kennedy's death, turnover in the White House staff occurred on a large scale and fairly rapidly.

The Office of Management and Budget (which, until 1970, was the Bureau of the Budget), on the other hand, contains mostly professional staff members. Only a few jobs at the top of the agency are open to presidential appointment. These jobs are extremely important and, if the president chooses his director and his few top assistants well, they can make a significant difference in the general orientation of the agency both toward their role in relation to the president and the operating agencies and toward the broad substance of policy. But the great bulk of the OMB staff continues from president to president and develops habitual ways of performing their duties and of interrelating with the rest of the government, including the president and the White House Office personnel.

The principal tasks of OMB include the preparation of the budget, the management of the spending of the money that is appropriated, coordination of executive-branch legislative proposals sent to Congress, improvement of the management of federal programs, and the collection of a wide range of information about federal programs both for general consumption by the public and the bureaucracy and for specific consumption by the president and his immediate staff.

The National Security Council has five statutory members: the president, vice-president, secretary of state, secretary of defense, and director of the Office of Emergency Preparedness. It also has a staff headed by an assistant to the president for national security affairs (the job held by Henry Kissinger until mid-1973). The formal council is used differently by different presidents. Eisenhower made it the overseer of some other formally established units and met with it regularly. Kennedy dismantled the Eisenhower machinery and rarely convened the formal council. Johnson used it more, although he still relied much more heavily on the staff than the council itself. Nixon meets with the formal council more often but the influence of the staff, and especially of Kissinger himself, hit an all-time high with him. The agenda for the council and the staff can include anything pertaining to national security. The NSC is also formally charged with overseeing the Central Intelligence Agency, a responsibility more apparent than real, since the CIA tends to behave with considerable autonomy, although President Nixon has displayed some desire to bring the CIA under more effective presidential control.

The Domestic Council was created in 1970 by President Nixon. It is supposed to parallel the National Security Council with respect to the whole range of domestic enterprises in which the national government is involved. In 1971 the membership of the council included the president, the vice-president, the attorney general, the secretary of commerce, the secretary of health, education, and welfare, the secretary of housing and urban development, the secretary of the interior, the secretary of labor, the secretary of transportation, the secretary of the treasury, the director and deputy director of the Office of Management and Budget, several counselors to the president, and an executive director. Given the large size of the council, the staff is almost inevitably the most important part of the operation, and the executive director is an especially critical adviser to the president. Virtually nothing in the domestic area is outside the purview of the council. The official statement of purpose in the *Government Organization Manual* makes this clear:

The purpose of the Council is to formulate and coordinate domestic policy recommendations to the president. The council assesses national needs and coordinates the establishment of national priorities; recommends integrated sets of policy choices; provides a rapid response to presidential needs for policy advice on pressing domestic issues; and maintains a continuous review of on-going programs from a policy standpoint.[13]

The Council of Economic Advisers has three academic economists as its statutory members (appointed by the president). Usually the chairman attains national visibility as a spokesman for the administration on economic matters. The staff contains a number of able economists. The staff advises the members, the rest of the executive office, and other agencies of the government on economic trends and assesses federal programs in relation to the economy. The major public document prepared by the CEA staff, the annual "Economic Message of the President," receives widespread public attention.

In the Nixon presidency the White House staff by 1973 had become dominant at the expense both of the Office of Management and Budget and a number of the cabinet secretaries. The legislative clearance function so central to the importance of the Office of Management and Budget became increasingly a White House function rather than a function of OMB.[14] The Nixon staff also made it difficult for close rapport to develop between the president and any of his cabinet members. It is certainly usual for a number of cabinet members to be relatively unimportant in the president's eyes, and the cabinet as a whole rarely develops any significant collective impact on the policy choices of the government. But it is rare for most of the departmental secretaries to be simultaneously upstaged by the White House staff. These relationships may change in post-Watergate readjustments, but it is clear that Nixon's personal preference is for a dominant White House.

---

[13] *U.S. Government Organization Manual, 1971–72* (Washington, D.C.: Government Printing Office, 1971), p. 63.

[14] Robert S. Gilmour, "Central Legislative Clearance: A Revised Perspective." *Public Administration Review*, vol. 31 (March/April, 1971), pp. 150–158.

TABLE 6-2. Growth of Central Presidential Staffs, 1954-1972

	Fiscal 1954 (Eisenhower)	Fiscal 1962 (Kennedy)	Fiscal 1967 (Johnson)	Fiscal 1972[a] (Nixon)
White House Office	246	273	250	540
Bureau of the Budget (Office of Management and Budget in 1972)	446	465	525	680
Council of Economic Advisers	26	44	48	57
National Security Council	29	50	48	75

Source: Compiled from data in the *Budget of the United States Government.* Appendices for Fiscal 1956, 1964, 1969, and 1973.

a. Figures for 1972 are estimates.

President Nixon has enhanced the importance of the White House office enormously. Simultaneously he has also been aggressive in increasing the size of the other central presidential staffs. Table 6–2 summarizes the growth of the central part of the Executive Office under the last four presidents. Nixon has fostered striking growth in the staff of all four components, with the White House staff being more than doubled. There was almost no growth in either the White House Office staff or the Bureau of the Budget during the Democrats' terms.

The President and Congress

The most critical relationship every president must work out if he is to attain his policy preferences is his personal and institutional relationship with Congress. This relationship can take a variety of forms.

A president's attitude toward his legislative role and his position on the activist-restraint spectrum help predict the likelihood of his legislative success—how far he can get with his domestic legislative program in Congress, assuming that Congress is controlled by his party. If the president stresses the potential for action in the office and acts as if the majority in Congress is a presidentially dominated majority, then his chances for legislative success are relatively good. If the president stresses the restraints on his office and acts as if the majority party in Congress is a congressionally dominant majority, then his chances for legislative success in terms of what he wants are relatively poor.

There are, of course, instances in which at least one house of Congress is controlled by a party other than the president's party. This situation has occurred in ten different Congresses (twenty years) in this century (1911–13, 1919–21, 1931–33, 1947–48, 1955–60, and 1969–74). Ordinarily, accommodations can be reached with respect to foreign policy in such a situation, but it is unusual for major developments to take place in the domestic sphere.

A study of ten Congresses scattered throughout the twentieth century suggests that the three kinds of majorities in Congress produce predictable patterns of relations between the leaders of that majority and the president, the degree of innovation in the techniques used by the leaders and the president to obtain their legislative preferences, the pattern of leadership organization in both houses of Congress, and the degree of legislative success as defined by the president and the leaders themselves.[15] Table 6–3 summarizes the findings of this study.

The Presidency: A Changing Institution

The basically changing nature of the presidency remains despite institutional developments that foreclose the option of total (or seemingly total) inactivity and passivity. Presidents still have lots of options about how to conduct themselves, the business of the office, and the business of the country. And,

[15] Randall B. Ripley, *Majority Party Leadership in Congress* (Boston: Little, Brown, 1969).

TABLE 6-3. The Relationships between Type of Majority and Nature of the Legislative Process and Results

Type of Majority	Character of Leader-President Relations	Degree of Innovation in Use of Techniques	Degree of Centralization in Leadership Pattern		Degree of Legislative Success
			House	Senate	
Presidential	Cooperation	High	High	High	High
Congressional	Mixed (mostly unsupported initiation)	Low	Varied	Low	Low
Truncated	Opposition	Varied	High	High	Low

Source: Randall B. Ripley, *Majority Party Leadership in Congress* (Boston: Little, Brown, 1969), p. 183. Reprinted with permission from Little, Brown.

fortunately for students of the office and citizens alike, presidents and presidential candidates talk about their conceptions of the office during campaigns, during incumbency, and after leaving the office. For example, in the 1968 campaign both Republican Richard Nixon and Democrat Hubert Humphrey articulated their basic notions of the office; not surprisingly, these notions differed. Their views are worth quoting at some length to give the flavor of the choices individual presidents can still make.

Humphrey, in a speech in Los Angeles on July 11, 1968, made the following statements:

> Whoever becomes President next January will discharge the traditional demands upon that office: To build consent, to magnify the people's conscience, to cause them to see what they might otherwise avoid, to recommend to Congress measures for the redress of grievances and injustices, and then fight for their passage, to conduct international discussions directed toward a more peaceful world, to counter threats to domestic tranquility and national security.
>
> He will face, as have few before him, the insistent demand *now* for one citizenship for all Americans—one birthright of freedom and opportunity to which all may claim equal inheritance.
>
> We shall know in our time whether this democratic ideal can be won—or whether America, despite her momentous achievements and her promise, will become another of history's false starts. . . .
>
> The next President will strive particularly to reach the people whose disappointment over America is keenest—including the most idealistic of our young people—because their basic hope for America is perhaps deepest.
>
> The next President must be America's teacher and leader—expressing our highest aspirations for justice and peace, at home or abroad. He must simultaneously be student and follower—learning from the people of their most profound hopes and their deepest concerns. . . .
>
> Our circumstances today call increasingly for an Open Presidency.
>
> Open in the sense of assuring the fullest possible use of that office to inform the American people of the problems and, even more, the prospects we face.
>
> Open in the sense of stimulating the frankest and widest

THE STRUCTURE OF GOVERNMENT

possible discussion and ventilation of America's problems—both inside and outside government.

Open in the sense of marshaling the spirit and mobilizing the energies of America to complete the attack on urban decay, illiteracy, unemployment, disease, hunger.

Open in the sense of a readiness to use the Presidency as the instrument not for the enlargement of the federal executive function, but the distribution of such responsibility to states and localities ready to accept it.

Open in the sense of greater access to all the people.

An Open Presidency must be a *strong* Presidency, one that draws its strength from direct and daily closeness to the people.[16]

Nixon, in a radio address on September 19, 1968, made the following statements:

The next President must unite America. He must calm its angers, ease its terrible frictions, and bring its people together once again in peace and mutual respect. He has to take hold of America before he can move it forward. . . . The first responsibility of leadership is to gain mastery over events, and to shape the future in the image of our hopes. The President today cannot stand aside from crisis; he cannot ignore division; he cannot simply paper over disunity. He must lead. . . .

The President is trusted (by the people), not to follow the fluctuations of the public-opinion polls, but to bring his own best judgment to bear on the best ideas his administration can muster. There are occasions on which a President must take unpopular measures. But his responsibility does not stop there. The President has a duty to decide, but the people have a right to know why. The President has a responsibility to tell them—to lay out all the facts, and to explain not only why he chose as he did but also what it means for the future. Only through an open, candid dialogue with the people can a President maintain his trust and leadership. . . .

And this brings me to another, related point: The President cannot isolate himself from the great intellectual ferments of his time. On the contrary, he must consciously and deliberately place himself at their center. The lamps of enlightenment are lit by the spark of controversy; their flames can be snuffed out by the blanket of consensus. . . .

[16] This quotation is taken from a 1968 campaign pamphlet entitled, "The Open Presidency."

   When we think of leadership, we commonly think of per-
suasion. But the coin of leadership has another side. In order
to lead, a President today must listen. . . . The President is
the only official who represents every American—rich and
poor, privileged and underprivileged. He represents those
whose misfortunes stand in domestic focus and also the great,
quiet, forgotten majority—the nonshouters and the nondem-
onstrators, the millions who ask principally to go their own
way in decency and dignity, and to have their own rights
accorded the same respect they accord the rights of others.
Only if he listens to the quiet voices can he be true to this
trust. This I pledge, that in a Nixon administration, America's citizens will not have to break the law to be heard, they
will not have to shout or resort to violence. We can restore
peace only if we make government attentive to the quiet as
well as the strident, and this I intend to do. . . .
   The Presidency is a place where priorities are set and goals
determined. We need a new attention to priorities, and a new
realism about goals. We are living today in a time of great
promise—but also of too many promises. . . . A President
must tell the people what cannot be done immediately as well
as what can. Hope is fragile, and too easily shattered by the
disappointment that follows inevitably on promises unkept
and unkeepable.[17]

Some similarities appear in these statements: they both talk
about listening, they both talk about leading, and, in effect,
they both talk about openness. There are, however, important
differences. An ideological difference emerges: on the one
hand, Humphrey stresses a presidentially led attack on economic problems and stresses his great sympathy for the young
disappointed with America; on the other hand, Nixon is wor-
ried about "too many promises" of action and is especially so-
licitous of the "great, quiet, forgotten majority." Nixon as
president has behaved quite consistently with the conception
he set forth in September, 1968. We can, of course, only speculate what a Humphrey presidency would have been like between 1969 and 1972, but it seems reasonable to suggest that
there would have been some major differences from the Nixon
presidency.

[17] This quotation is taken from excerpts of a radio speech printed in
Congressional Quarterly Weekly Report (September 27, 1968), p. 2549.

There is also a tension built into the presidency in terms of the potential for autocratic action contained in the office as opposed to the forces striving for popular or democratic control of the office. Both the autocratic elements in the office and the democratic elements in it serve the country well in some respects; but both kinds of elements also contain some dangers.

Autocracy is obviously dangerous in that it may allow the president to abuse power, restrict individual rights, lead the country into unwise foreign adventures, and so on. Yet, some autocratic elements may be necessary for the president to move swiftly (particularly when dealing with foreign policy) or perhaps to move at all (even on domestic matters).

Complete democratic control and responsiveness may be dangerous in that it may lead the president in harmful ways (what if the popular will demands nuclear war with China or repression of blacks?) or it may simply prevent him from moving at all if there are violent and close divisions. However, a large measure of democratic control and responsiveness is useful and desirable: presumably citizens should have a say in their own destiny and in the destiny of their nation, even if they choose unwisely.

In the American system the only direct popular control on the president is the election itself. Then there are the other pressures of public opinion—both direct and those channeled through parties and interest groups. There are also the pressures of the other organs of government—state and local units in the federal system, the bureaucracy, Congress, and the courts. These are only indirect elements of popular control; nevertheless, they do represent important restraints.

The main chances for the president to expand his autocratic domain come during times of crisis: war, internal violence, economic collapse. In normal times a President who is inclined to be activist is constantly encountering limits, although these are clearly not all popular limits.

CHAPTER 7

The Bureaucracy

The federal bureaucracy makes war; it also decides which truck line will carry plate glass from Pittsburgh to Richmond. It directs the space program; it also conducts research into the causes of cancer. Parts of the federal bureaucracy are involved in administering every governmental program and piece of legislation.

The bureaucracy is a mammoth enterprise of nearly three million civilian employees. It has no single head, although theoretically the president is responsible for setting general policy and directing the efforts of the bureaucracy. Although it is usually discussed as if it were a single entity, the bureaucracy is not a monolith. In reality it is a very complex combination of government agencies administering a wide variety of complex programs. The mode of operation, the norms of behavior, and the general ethos vary from agency to agency. Sometimes the parts of the bureaucracy pull together, and sometimes they pull in opposite directions.

141

The average citizen usually knows very little about the bureaucracy because most of the time its actions are part of a daily routine that does not warrant special attention. In those instances when people do take note of the bureaucracy it is often due to a negative stimulus—the Social Security Administration sends a check to a wrong address, or the Internal Revenue Service audits a tax return.

This chapter will attempt to portray the importance of the bureaucracy as it functions to produce policy statements, actions, and results.

Programmatic Impact of the Bureaucracy on Society

The bureaucracy administers a very large number of programs that have a variety of impacts on both the general public and on a whole range of special publics (clienteles for individual programs). Several general propositions about the impact of these programs can be made.

First, individual programs are capable of extremely rapid growth in terms of policy statements and actions. In such growth periods, however, the bureaucracy may have considerable trouble achieving desired policy results. The bureaucracy is capable of moving with relative swiftness to meet perceived problems and needs. This is obviously true of programs in fields such as defense or space, where significant external events—such as a Russian or Chinese military move or the Russian launching of a space satellite—demand swift responses. But it can also be true of less visible, more domestically oriented programs.

It should also be noted that, viewed year by year, especially in terms of dollar budget, the growth or shrinkage of any specific program may appear to be small and incremental. Viewed over a slightly longer span of time, however, growth often no longer appears incremental, but quite substantial and rapid. (Shrinkage of a program is more likely to proceed slowly, however.)

The basic social-security program—old age and survivors

insurance—provides an example of rapid growth in a program in terms of all three kinds of policy responses. Presidents and Congresses both said they were going to increase benefits and coverage and did so. And beneficiaries in fact received substantial increases, thus presumably increasing their self-reliance and dignity. In 1950 only one-quarter of Americans over sixty-five received social-security benefits. By early 1966 eighty-five percent of persons over sixty-five were covered and receiving benefits. Another five percent received pensions under other federal programs for civil servants and railroad employees. In 1965, ninety-seven percent of all persons turning sixty-five were eligible for social security.[1] Table 7–1 shows the vast growth in money resources allocated to this program in past years and indicates that such growth will continue in future years.

A view of the factors involved in a large-scale change in a program is afforded by the Social Security Administration after the passage of the social-security amendments in 1965.

TABLE 7-1. Status of Old-Age and Survivors Insurance Trust Fund (in Billions of Dollars)

Calendar Year	Contributions	Benefit Payments
1951	3.4	1.9
1955	5.7	5.0
1960	10.9	10.7
1965	16.0	15.6
1970	25.4	23.4
1980	35.0	31.6
1990	40.0	40.3
2000	46.4	45.0
2020	56.0	62.2

Source: Advisory Council on Social Security, *The Status of the Social Security Program and Recommendations for Its Improvement* (1965), pp. 109-10.

[1] These data come from Robert M. Ball, "Policy Issues in Social Security." Address at the annual meeting of the American Society for Public Administration (April 14, 1966).

The law was signed July 30, 1965. It made two basic changes in the Social Security Act: an increase in benefits and the creation of a program of medical care for those over sixty-five.[2]

The magnitude of the first change was great. It meant that a program geared to disburse 18.8 billion dollars in 1967 would now have to disburse 24.9 billlion dollars. One change in benefits to children of deceased, disabled, and retired workers involved the collection of about half a million applications within a few months time.

The magnitude of the medicare program was even greater. The program had two major parts, a basic compulsory hospital insurance program and a voluntary medical insurance program. Three major efforts had to be mounted by the Social Security Administration immediately. First, the responsible officials had to get applications from potential beneficiaries and had to determine their eligibility. This meant contacting nineteen million people within an eight-month period by a variety of personal and mass communications. Second, social-security officials had to get the providers of service and the administrative agents to be used for the hospital-insurance program ready to perform their functions. This involved contacting 10,000 hospitals, 15,000 nursing homes, and 1,000 home-health agencies. Third, the government had to prepare those involved in the voluntary program for the beginning of the program. This meant contacting all doctors in private practice and deciding what administrative agents to use for the program. One hundred and forty organizations applied to be administrative agents for various parts of the program; forty-nine were chosen.

The above changes illustrate the ability of the bureaucracy to move quickly to implement new statutory authority. This does not mean, of course, that all such movement will be efficient.

A second proposition about the effect of executive-branch programs on the public is that a program does not do just one

[2] Data for this discussion come from Robert M. Ball, "A Report on the Implementation of the 1965 Amendments to the Social Security Act as of March 15, 1966" (Unpublished report).

thing. A single program can have a wide variety of policy results or impacts, including some not initially anticipated by Congress or executive officials. For example, Title I of the Elementary and Secondary School Assistance Act (1965) provided about a billion dollars annually aimed at helping impoverished students already enrolled in both public and private grade and high schools. The method of extending this help was not prescribed, however, and it could include, according to a perceptive newspaper account, "health tests, school breakfasts, cultural trips, clothing, family counseling and psychiatric help, as well as classroom instruction."[3]

Third, most important fields in which the government seeks specified policy results involve programs (representing statements and actions) administered by a large number of agencies. Shared administration is the norm in the federal government. In the health field, for example, although over seventy percent of the budget is handled by the Department of Health, Education, and Welfare, a variety of other agencies make important policy statements and actions in the health field. Table 7–2 summarizes federal outlays for health in fiscal year 1971 by agency. These outlays went for such things as research, various training and education programs, construction of health facilities, direct and indirect programs in support of hospitals and other medical services, and various disease prevention and control programs. This general pattern of administration may seem inefficient in that it fosters some jurisdictional disputes, jealousy, and redundancy of effort. However, it also can promote healthy competition, innovation, and experimentation.

Fourth, the budget offers the single most important index to government action, because it provides some gross limits within which action must take place. Monetary amounts are important because they set the boundaries beyond which an agency cannot go. They provide the latitude within which an agency must attempt to have its impact on society. Thus, the proposals by the bureaucracy and president to Congress (through the

[3] *Wall Street Journal* (April 19, 1966).

THE STRUCTURE OF GOVERNMENT

TABLE 7-2. Federal Outlays for Health Programs by Agency, Fiscal 1971

Agency	Millions of Dollars	Percent of Health Budget
Department of Health, Education, and Welfare	14,490.2	71.8%
Department of Defense	2,121.1	10.5%
Veterans Administration	2,034.8	10.1%
Department of Agriculture	219.8	1.1%
Office of Economic Opportunity	187.2	0.9%
Agency for International Development	147.2	0.7%
Department of Labor	137.1	0.7%
Atomic Energy Commission	117.2	0.6%
Other[a]	723.2	3.6%
Total Outlays	20,177.8	100.0%

Source: Compiled from data in *Special Analyses, Budget of the United States Government for Fiscal 1973*, p. 176.

a. This includes the Environmental Protection Agency, the Department of Housing and Urban Development, the Civil Service Commission, the Department of State, the National Science Foundation, NASA, and some other agencies, as well as agency contributions to health funds.

Office of Management and Budget) and Congress' response in the form of appropriations and other grants of money are at the heart of the policy process in the federal government.

In the last two decades budget outlays by the federal government have fluctuated between 17.2 percent and 21.6 percent of the gross national product.[4] Thus, as a general rule it can be said that the government spends about one-fifth of the total value of goods and services produced in the nation. The bureaucracy's functions have not remained static, however, nor has the relative importance of various agencies within the bureaucracy remained constant. Moreover, the total size of the government's program has also grown. Table 7-3 illustrates through budget figures the overall growth of government. Al-

[4] *The Budget of the United States Government, Fiscal Year 1972* (Washington. D.C.: Government Printing Office, 1971), p. 575.

TABLE 7-3. Growth of the Federal Budget, 1900-1970

Fiscal Year	Budget Outlays (in Millions of Dollars)	Percentage Change from Previous Five-Year Period
1900	521	- - -
1905	567	+9%
1910	694	+22%
1915	746	+7%
1920	6,358	+752%
1925	2,924	−54%
1930	3,320	+14%
1935	6,497	+96%
1940	9,589	+48%
1945	95,184	+893%
1950	43,147	−55%
1955	68,509	+59%
1960	92,223	+35%
1965	118,430	+28%
1970	196,588	+66%

Source: Adapted from *The Budget of the United States Government, Fiscal Year 1972*, p. 576.

though the size of the government's budget in relation to the GNP has remained relatively stable since 1945, the absolute amount of the budget has increased enormously. Particularly dramatic have been the spurts associated with World Wars I and II and the cold war.

The budget is a statement of governmental priorities. Given limited resources (and even a budget over 200 billion dollars a year is based on limited resources) the executive branch and Congress must both make choices: should defense get seventy or seventy-five billion dollars; should aid to education be ten billion or twelve billion dollars; should legal assistance for the poor be included at all?

The priorities of the government change over time. Any total budget is, in general, only slightly different from the budget that immediately precedes it. But over the period of a few years these incremental and gradual changes can be significant. Table 7–4 presents data on the changing shape of the federal budget by functional categories between 1945 and 1970.

TABLE 7-4. Budget Outlays by Function, 1945-1970 (in Billions of Dollars)

Function	1945	1950	Fiscal Year 1955	1960	1965	1970
National Defense	85.7	30.4	58.7	49.8	41.9	40.8
Education and Manpower	0.2	0.5	0.8	1.1	1.9	3.7
Health	0.2	0.6	0.4	0.8	1.5	6.6
Income Security	1.2	10.9	13.3	19.7	21.7	22.3
Veterans' Benefits and Services	1.2	20.5	6.6	5.9	4.8	4.4
Agriculture and Rural Development	1.7	6.5	5.9	3.6	4.1	3.2
Natural Resources	0.3	2.9	0.7	1.1	1.7	1.3
Commerce and Transportation	4.4	3.9	1.6	5.2	6.2	4.7
Community Development and Housing	a	0.6	a	1.1	0.2	1.5
International Affairs and Finance	3.5	11.1	3.0	3.3	3.7	1.8
Space Research and Technology	a	0.1	0.1	0.4	4.3	1.9
Total Budget Outlays	95.2	43.1	68.5	92.2	118.4	196.6

Source: Adapted from *The Budget of the United States Government, Fiscal Year 1973*, p. 75-76.

a. Less than 0.05.

The 1945 budget was, of course, skewed toward defense expenditures because of the heavy spending necessitated by World War II. Between 1950 and 1970 several trends appear clearly. Space research and technology, health, and education and manpower appear as the functions that received the strongest new emphases. Relative de-emphases have been given to agriculture, natural resources, veterans' benefits and services, and international affairs and finance.

The Fiscal 1973 budget presented by President Nixon in early 1972 is summarized in Table 7–5 in order to show the

TABLE 7-5. The Federal Budget: Outlays by Function, Fiscal 1973[a]

Function	Billions of Dollars	Percent of Total Budget
National Defense	78,310	31.8%
Income Security	69,658	28.3%
Health	18,117	7.4%
Veterans' Benefits and Services	11,745	4.8%
Communication and Transportation	11,550	4.7%
Education and Manpower	11,281	4.6%
Agriculture and Rural Development	6,891	2.8%
Community Development and Housing	4,844	2.0%
International Affairs and Finance	3,844	1.6%
Space Research and Technology	3,191	1.3%
Natural Resources and Environment	2,450	1.0%
Other	24,377	9.8%
Total Outlays	246,257	100.1%[b]

Source: *The Budget of the United States Government, Fiscal Year 1973,* p. 73.

a. These are estimates for 1973.
b. Does not total to 100 because of rounding.

current priorities of the government. By far the two largest expenditures go for national defense (military construction, procurement, and salaries) and income security (principally social-security payments).

The Consequences of Program Decisions for Bureaucratic Agencies

A set of general propositions can also be made about the impact of government programs on the federal agencies themselves. These propositions are important because internal developments in the agencies can help determine the nature of subsequent statements and actions by those agencies.

First, some fields necessitate the participation of many agencies, especially when a number of specific programs are mounted. This necessity increases the chance of interagency competition, jealousy, and conflict—developments that may reduce the ability of the agencies to achieve desired results. An additional consequence of having a function spread over many agencies is that interagency committees become necessary as a means of attempting to coordinate the undertaking. When programs seem to require the presence of interagency committees, these committees will often become the actual decision makers for the program, although the responsibility for administering it may reside elsewhere. Thus, in the foreign-aid program, for example, most of the funds are actually programmed by interagency committees.[5]

Second, some agencies can become involved in unintended areas of activity. This may also cause jealousy and competition on the part of other agencies. For example, the Economic Development Administration of the Department of Commerce, created in 1965, was given a heavy rural bias. Urban development was supposed to be left to the Department of Housing and Urban Development, also created in 1965. Yet EDA took the opening that was left to it in the urban field and developed

[5] See Randall B. Ripley, "Interagency Committees and Incrementalism: The Case of Aid to India," *Midwest Journal of Political Science*, vol. 8 (May 1964), pp. 143–65.

a major program for two urban areas (Oakland and Brooklyn). Not only was this running the possibility of encroaching on HUDs field of activity, but the program was also heavily involved in a civil-rights effort. In Oakland, for example, new jobs created by the program had to be filled giving priority to blacks. EDA arranged to become more intimately involved in corporate hiring practices than any federal agency up to that time. Clearly this effort ran the risk of raising eyebrows in the Justice Department and the Civil Rights Commission, as well as other agencies more normally involved in civil-rights activities.[6]

Third, rapid growth in old agencies can cause major and disruptive internal changes through introducing new employees, procedures, and organizational arrangements that are particularly threatening to longtime employees wedded to their customary ways of conducting business. The Public Health Service budget, for example, was increased almost ten-fold (from 250 million to 2.4 billion dollars) between 1954 and 1966. Expansion during this period was accompanied by two major reorganizations, in 1960 and again in 1966. The 1960 reorganization generated a major internal struggle.[7]

The Office of Education in HEW went through some of the same kind of inner turmoil at the end of a period of rapid growth. In 1950 it employed only 300 people and had a budget of 40 million dollars. By 1962 it had 1400 employees and a budget of 600 million dollars. The budget for 1967 called for an expenditure of 2.6 billion dollars. From the late 1950s until the mid-1960s the agency underwent a series of changes that made many of the old-time employees unhappy, but presumably left the agency in a better position to meet its new responsibilities.[8]

---

[6] *Wall Street Journal* (April 25, 1966).

[7] On the events in 1960 see Edith Carper, *The Reorganization of the Public Health Service*, Inter-University Case Program #89 (Indianapolis, Ind.: Bobbs-Merrill, 1965). On the events in 1966 see the *Washington Post* (April 26, 1966) and the *Evening Star* (Washington, D.C.: April 26, 1966).

[8] See Stephen K. Bailey, *The Office of Education and the Education Act of 1965*, Inter-University Case Program #100 (Indianapolis, Ind.: Bobbs-Merrill, 1966).

Fourth, it is easier for new agencies to absorb rapid growth than it is for established agencies, but the survival of a new agency is more tenuous. New agencies given large programs to administer on the day of their creation are likely to be filled with enthusiasm, and they are not saddled with entrenched personnel who oppose change. But, unless the necessity of their task is patently obvious both in Congress and in the executive branch (including the presidency) they may find themselves lacking the support from outside clients or within officialdom necessary to withstand attacks on their continued existence, at least at high levels of funding. Many of the New Deal agencies suffered from insufficient outside support, as well as from the natural confusion that accompanies the mounting of new large-scale efforts. In recent years the Office of Economic Opportunity—the general staff for the war on poverty—has been beset by the same problems. It has not been able, for a variety of reasons, to build a stable, supportive constituency. The president himself proposed termination of OEO in 1973. If OEO succumbs, however, it is likely that the functions it performs will survive in other, well-established agencies. Both agencies and programs are ultimately dependent on sufficient political support.

The National Aeronautics and Space Administration, on the other hand, came into being, grew rapidly, and had no serious political problems for the first decade of its existence, probably because few were willing to question the need for massive space activities and a single space agency to supervise them. By the late 1960s, however, its funding and public support both began to shrink as space exploration simultaneously achieved some specified goals (especially the goal of putting men on the moon) and lost a large part of its glamour.

Patterns of Administration and Program Impact

Federal programs can be administered in a variety of patterns. The choice of which pattern to use for a given program is important in helping to determine what impact the program can and cannot have on the intended beneficiaries (or target populations) and on society in general.

Virtually all of the domestic programs of the federal government require some form of geographical decentralization and they may also involve some form of involvement of state and local units of government or parts of the private sector or both. Four basic variants of administrative patterns for domestic programs of the federal government are presented in Figure 7–1.

In pattern I the Washington office of the agency is all-important. It makes virtually all decisions, and distributes the benefits (symbolized by a dollar sign in the figure). Its field offices are principally transmission agencies for the benefits. The beneficiaries are treated the same throughout the nation; no discretion is left with the field offices to treat them differently. This pattern might be labeled *centralization*. (The other three patterns are all variations of *decentralization*.) An example of a program administered in this way is the social-security program.

In pattern II the Washington office is still important. It sends both directions of a general sort and benefits to be distributed to its field offices. But the field offices retain considerable power of decision and they exercise that power in addition to passing on the benefits to the clients. Their power is such that, although the target population is defined in Washington, regional variations in the exact treatment accorded that population can and do occur. The Environmental Protection Agency operates in this fashion.

In pattern III the Washington office is primarily important only as a source of federal dollars. It also issues standards that are supposed to guide the various state and local governmental units (as contrasted to the federal units in patterns I and II) that serve as the field establishment. But often these standards are unclear, badly communicated, or so broad as to have no practical effect. The state and local governmental units themselves become the primary decision makers both about the distribution of benefits and the conditions under which benefits will be granted or denied. Thus, although the legislation

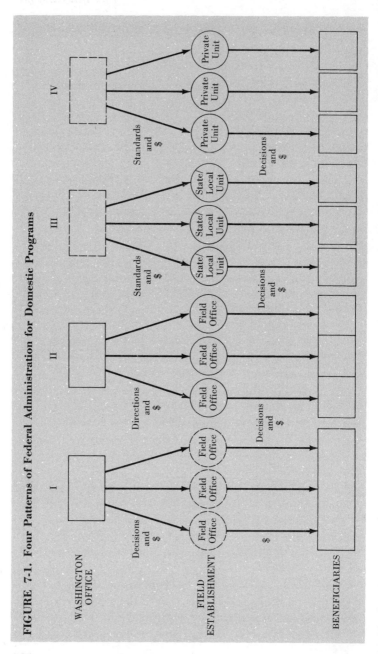

FIGURE 7-1. Four Patterns of Federal Administration for Domestic Programs

154

authorizing the program may in theory define a national target population, in practice there are a number of different target populations that can have very different characteristics from city to city and state to state. The revenue-sharing legislation passed late in 1972 seems to open up the possibility that a number of federal programs will, in effect, become a collection of state and local programs and thus approximate pattern III. In the past, part of the urban-renewal program was administered this way.

In pattern IV the Washington office is again primarily a source of money and standards that are likely to be vague. Now the field establishments are not governmental at all but are instead private. These units pass on benefits after making the basic decisions about who gets what benefits under what conditions. Thus, once again the beneficiaries are treated not as a single population but as a collection of different populations united only by sharing in the same program, but not necessarily by any other important characteristics. Examples of this type of administration include the Community Action Program of the poverty program (at least in theory) and a variety of programs from the Agriculture Department in which committees of farmers become decision-making units.

The Bureaucracy and Its Clients

Virtually every agency in the federal bureaucracy has an identifiable clientele in the private sector. By *clientele* is meant those individuals, groups, organizations, and institutions that stand to benefit, either directly or indirectly, from the programs of any given agency. Table 7–6 summarizes the vast private sector clientele for only one federal department— Health, Education, and Welfare.

Clients are important to agencies because they can both give needed support as the agencies seek funds and personnel from the Office of Management and Budget and from Congress, and they can also withhold that support. In addition, they can often provide agency officials with valuable feedback on how

155

TABLE 7-6. Private-Sector Clientele for HEW Programs

HEW Program	Private-Sector Clients
Food and Drug Administration	Regulated industries Professional associations 15 HEW advisory groups
Health Services and Mental Health Administration	Medical and dental schools Hospitals Voluntary health organizations Mental-health community 68 HEW advisory groups
National Institutes of Health	Research organizations Science community Health professional students 202 HEW advisory groups
Social and Rehabilitation Service	12 million welfare recipients Welfare-rights groups Vocational rehabilitation groups Nursing-home operations American Public Welfare Association 29 HEW advisory groups
Social Security Administration	26 million beneficiaries 94 million contributors Hospitals Life-insurance firms Organized labor 4 HEW advisory groups
Office of Education	Colleges and universities Education industry Civil-rights groups American Federation of Teachers National Education Association 22 HEW advisory groups

Source: Adapted from the *National Journal*, vol. 2 (September 12, 1970), pp. 1980-81.

well the programs of the agency are being administered from the point of view of the recipients.

Some agencies may have a clientele that is relatively homogeneous and highly issue specific. Other agencies have diverse clienteles, the components of which do not conflict. Other agencies (particularly larger ones with numerous programs) may have diverse clienteles in which the various components do have competing and conflicting interests.

In general, clients create a powerful force for the status quo (with its normal incremental growth) in any given area. These programs with stronger clientele are more secure from attack designed to limit or shrink them than those programs with weaker clientele. Foreign-aid programs, for example, are relatively vulnerable because most of their clients are foreign and do not have much weight in the normal policy process within the U.S. government.

Some clienteles are well-established and have existed for a long period of time with relatively little change. For example, the whole network of farm groups and governmentally sponsored committees of farmers have long dominated the policy process for a whole range of agricultural-support programs.

When the government enters a new field of endeavor, a constituency will develop for that endeavor, drawing clients from among the supporters who may have worked for the adoption of some particular piece of authorizing legislation, as well as from groups who support the existence and growth of a new program out of reasons of self-interest. Daniel Greenberg, a well-known writer on science affairs, describes the clientele that emerged around NASA and the space program in general:

> Space, like civil rights, veterans' benefits, or urban renewal, has now become a well-rooted part of the American landscape. . . . It has its own politics, its own economics, and its own congressional champions. . . .
>
> As this money [the money spent on the program] went out into the American economy, space developed a constituency that, in terms of economic and political self-interest, dwarfs the lately arrived opposition. . . .
>
> The breadth and depth of this constituency are illustrated by a few statistics which, though open to question in some cases, leave no doubt that the plan to land a man on the moon has become a critical economic factor in the lives of an extremely large number of people. According to NASA testi-

157

mony before Congress, 300,000 persons will be employed on Apollo by next year; 31 states received NASA prime contract awards in excess of $1 million last year; of these states, eight received awards of over $50 million each. In fiscal 1963, NASA provided $73 million in grants and contracts to 139 universities, including many institutions which were largely ignored by other federal granting agencies, and which therefore have sound reasons for gratitude to NASA.[9]

A more unusual example involves a business-oriented clientele for so-called New Society programs under the Johnson Administration. These domestic programs, aimed at the poorer classes in society, could be expected to get little ideological support among the business community. Nevertheless, the practical economic implications of the program produced a sizable business group supporting them.

Many federal programs have client groups built into the decision process—through a variety of advisory bodies and committees of beneficiaries. One survey in 1971 revealed more than 3200 such committees scattered throughout the government. It has been asserted that "Most of those committees are stacked in favor of special interests."[10] In many fields of endeavor the line between public enterprise and private enterprise is faint, with personnel and information crossing the supposed boundary routinely.

Every government agency also has to deal with many other governmental units. These units are not clients in the private sector but do represent other important institutions and individuals with which the agency must deal. For example, the Department of Health, Education, and Welfare is subjected to demands, requests, and pressures from a vast array of other governmental units. Within the Executive Office of the President the Office of Management and Budget, the Council of Economic Advisers, the Domestic Affairs Council, and domestic staff members in the White House Office all have numerous

[9] Daniel S. Greenberg, "Space: Formidable Political Base Overshadows Attempts to Revise Administration's Lunar Program," *Science* (July 10, 1964), p. 137.

[10] Robert W. Dietsch, "The Invisible Bureaucracy," *New Republic* (Feb. 20, 1971), p. 19.

dealings with the department and its various parts. Programs in the Departments of Justice, Housing and Urban Development, Labor, Agriculture, and Interior and in the Office of Economic Opportunity and the Veterans Administration deal with issues of importance to HEW and thus necessitate a number of inter-departmental committees, meetings, and decisions.

Eight committees of the House of Representatives and eight committees of the Senate oversee various parts of the HEW programs. HEW is also constantly interacting with the court system in welfare and school desegregation cases.

The Bureaucracy and Congress

The relations between the federal bureaucracy and Congress are extremely important because it is within this relationship that most policy and program decisions are made.

The federal bureaucracy is often portrayed as eclipsing Congress as a policy-making organ. New ideas and technical expertise are seen to reside almost exclusively in the executive branch. Depending on one's point of view this development is either praised or bemoaned. The real situation is not so simple. Certainly, the federal bureaucracy has been growing in size. It has also been growing in its grasp of extremely technical matters. At the same time it has been trying to organize itself internally so that it can approach Congress more effectively in support of the policies and programs it desires.

Several factors have, however, allowed Congress to retain much of its importance in relation to specific policies and programs. First, Congress has some powers granted to it by the Constitution that are, by nature, important and that cannot be diminished or removed by the executive branch, no matter how aggressive and skilled it may be.

Second, Congress has also increased its grasp of technically complex programs. Congressional staff has improved both in quality and in quantity over the past two decades. Some individual senators and representatives can also become quite expert in specialized subjects, often more so than the political appointee heading an executive-branch department or agency.

Third, because the executive branch is not a monolith, there are numerous differences of opinion within it. Members of the House and Senate can magnify their influence in the policy process by aligning themselves with a specific side in a policy dispute within the executive branch.

Fourth, in many ways Congress and the bureaucracy co-operate much more than they conflict. To view them as fierce competitors on every issue or even on very many issues is unrealistic. On most matters they are searching for a mutually agreeable solution to a problem or set of problems that they view in much the same way. Technical experts in the bureaucracy will sometimes work for congressional committees on loan from their agencies.

THE ROLE OF THE LEGISLATIVE PROGRAM OF THE PRESIDENT

As discussed in the chapter on the presidency, the legislative program of the president has evolved in this century, and of necessity the members of various departments and agencies play a large role in framing this program. The president's legislative program is so large and complex that the presidential staff cannot possibly rely solely on its own knowledge and judgment in putting it together. Departments develop legislative programs out of which they choose their highest priority and largest items for possible inclusion in the presidential program. The Office of Management and Budget plays the principal institutional role in assembling the program, choosing among alternatives offered by departments and agencies, and reconciling logical conflicts between what the various parts of the bureaucracy desire.

Once the program of the president has been formulated and made public, subsequent departmental or agency proposals for legislative action are weighed against the priorities and specifics of the total program by OMB. Virtually every congressional committee routinely sends every bill to departments and agencies affected, as well as to OMB, for their opinions. The judgment of OMB always includes a statement of whether the proposal is in accord with the program of the president, and naturally this gives the president magnified legislative influence.

Any department or agency that wants to submit its own bill to Congress must first have the bill cleared by OMB. If the bill is labeled as not in accord with the program of the president, the agency cannot submit it formally as an agency proposal. An enterprising bureaucrat stopped by OMB can "bootleg" the bill to Congress by having a sympathetic congressman or senator introduce it himself, but the bill would not have the official sanction of the institutional presidency.

DEPARTMENTAL LIAISON

In the two decades following World War II, all of the federal departments and most of the large independent agencies created offices of congressional liaison. Prior to that time only the military services had formal operations in this field. This development was actively promoted by the various post-war presidents, especially President Eisenhower, who had had experience in army liaison work and saw the great utility of the operation.

The tasks that the liaison officials perform include representation of department or agency positions in formal testimony on Capitol Hill; representation of these positions in informal contacts and discussion with party leaders, committee chairmen, and rank-and-file members; preparation of formal testimony for other departmental officials; answering senators' and representatives' inquiries and those from their constituents; and (depending on the agency) participation in policy development within the agency.

The scale of agency and departmental liaison operations has increased greatly in the last ten years. In 1963, for example, the ten departments of the executive branch spent almost two million man-hours replying to requests from members and committees of both houses and preparing agency material for presentation to Congress. The departments had 500 people working in liaison and the total costs of their informational efforts exceeded five million dollars. When the principal independent agencies are added, over 700 people worked in liaison by 1963 and the cost was almost eight million dollars. By 1965, the Defense Department alone employed 383 persons directly involved in congressional liaison and spent almost three and one-half million dollars.

JOINT DEVELOPMENT OF POLICIES AND PROGRAMS

Thus far, the discussion has concentrated on the impact of the bureaucracy on Congress. But this relationship is two-way: Congress also has an important impact on the bureaucracy.

One way in which Congress affects the bureaucracy is by participating in the development of policies and programs. Congress does not merely react to what the bureaucracy presents it. Instead, it often participates in framing the alternatives among which both it and the executive branch must choose. Naturally, the impact of Congress varies from area to area. In some areas, the bureaucracy clearly takes the initiative. In others, the major initiative comes from the bureaucracy, but Congress also makes an input. And in a few areas, the major initiative comes from Congress.

At one end of the spectrum (the executive end), for example, is the war on poverty. This was conceived, developed, and put in legislative language in the executive branch. Key congressmen and senators were certainly important as supporters of the executive's ideas, but they were not important as initiators.

At the other end of the spectrum (the congressional end), for example, is legislation on air and power pollution that has been passed in the last several decades. Here the major ideas of what needed doing often came from congressional staff members or from key senators or representatives themselves. They were in the position of soliciting support from the executive branch, rather than the other way around.

CONGRESSIONAL OVERSIGHT OF ADMINISTRATION

Congress can magnify its policy impact by aggressive oversight of bureaucratic activities. Congress not only enacts laws, but it also must make sure that they are faithfully executed. Congress must not only guarantee the honesty of administration (which is important, too, of course), but, more important, it must devise ways of making sure that its impact does not cease once a law is enacted. When Congress passes a law the chief supporters of that law in the House and Senate usually have firm ideas of what the law should do, what problems it should reach, and how it should be administered. If it is administered so that the desired goals are not attained, most Senators and Representatives want to have some levers to force an adjustment of administrative practices, patterns, and procedures so that the goal can be achieved.

Through the years Congress has developed a number of specific techniques that give it the leverage it seeks. The most important of these techniques are discussed below.

First, and most important, Congress, of course, possesses monetary power. If an agency or department is not administering laws the way in which congressmen want them administered, presumably that agency or department can be deprived of funds for its other programs until it comes around to the congressional point of view. Or additional funds, earmarked for the function that is thought to be neglected, can be given to the agency.

Second, the structure of the executive branch is subject to change (or prevention of change) by Congress. Congress has delegated much of this power to the president, which is quite proper, but has usually retained at least a legislative veto over reorganization plans submitted by the president. And it can take the initiative in shifting specific functions and agencies as it did, for example, by shifting the water pollution control agency from Health, Education, and Welfare to the Department of the Interior.

Third, federal personnel are subject to congressional power. In the various civil-service statutes Congress can place grade and type of personnel limits that affect program administration. If a scientific program is thought to be neglected, for example, Congress can remove some of the limits on hiring of scientific personnel.

Fourth, the congressional investigative power has often been used to highlight and either criticize or praise specific bureaucratic practices in administering certain programs.

We can summarize the relationship between Congress and the bureaucracy in three statements:

1. The points of contact between the bureaucracy and Congress are numerous. There is much personal interchange between members and staff members on Capitol Hill and civil servants and political appointees in the executive branch.

2. In recent years the executive branch has formalized its efforts to influence congressional decision making, especially through the expanding role of OMB in legislative clearance and through the increasingly important departmental liaison efforts.

3. Congress has not become, however, a passive reflector of the wishes of the bureaucrats. Members of both houses make important inputs of their own in the policy process. And Congress as an institution maintains extremely important powers that allow it to have influence on the way in which the bureaucracy conducts the business of government.

CHAPTER 8

Congress

The Congress of the United States is the most powerful national legislative body in the developed countries of the world. Virtually everything that the government does is reviewed, at least in part, by Congress. The review can take a number of different forms, ranging from just talk to very painstaking attention to the details of public spending.

Many subjects involving Congress have been researched in great detail and reported on in a wide variety of books and articles. This chapter will focus on the congressional impact on public policy, a subject that has received somewhat less attention than internal politics, personalities, and procedures. First, the general functions performed by Congress that are policy relevant will be discussed. Second, the pressures on individual members as they seek to make up their minds on policy questions will be summarized. Third, the role of political parties as the primary link between Congress and both the voters and the policy wishes of the president will be outlined.

Fourth, attention will be paid to the specific policy-related activities of the formal party leaders in Congress. Finally, some elements of the qualitative impact of congressional committees will be assessed.

The Policy-Related Functions of Congress

Congress performs a variety of functions, but one can be viewed as overarching: it helps, or at least tries to help, resolve societal conflict. If it is largely successful in the performance of this function and if the other institutions of society are also largely successful in performing the same function, then society is likely to be relatively stable. If Congress and the other institutions of government are unsuccessful in resolving conflict, then societal instability may develop. Failure is, of course, possible; the American Civil War provides a classic example of what happens when societal conflict cannot be resolved through normal channels.

Despite the ultimate importance of this overarching function, it does not have much analytical utility. Rather, there are four more specific categories for ordering the discussion of the policy-relevant functions of Congress: (1) lawmaking, (2) oversight of administration, (3) education of the public, and (4) representation. These categories do not include everything Congress does that can affect society, but they do include those functions central to congressional impact on public policy (thus, for example, the limited judicial function of Congress is omitted) and those functions that can be consciously and directly manipulated by members of the two houses (Congress' leadership selection function—most dramatically for presidential candidates—is, for example, omitted because although important its performance is largely determined by events and circumstances outside the control of the specific preferences and actions of senators and representatives).

Congress has great latitude in performing these four functions. The institution we call Congress is principally the collection of individuals happening to serve in it at any given time.

166

The wishes and preferences of those members and the behavior based on those wishes and preferences can make a real difference in how the functions are performed. Some outer limits of congressional behavior may be immutably fixed but they are far from confining; the range of congressional choice in the performance of these functions is great.

CONGRESS AND LAWMAKING

The growth of government activity described in Chapter 1 has been reflected by the increasing scope of congressional activity in the past one hundred years. Prior to the Civil War, congressional lawmaking activity in the domestic sphere was basically limited to promoting the development of the nation. This sort of interest has, of course, persisted to the present day, and Congress is still heavily involved in the subsidy of a wide range of private development activities.

By the latter part of the nineteenth century Congress became involved in questions of regulation of railroads and trusts. Since that time congressional concern with regulation has greatly expanded to include such diverse matters as unfair business practices, all modes of transportation, power, radio and television, food and drugs, labor relations, and the securities market.

At roughly the time of the Great Depression, Congress also began to get heavily involved in a conscious way in the redistribution of the economic and social benefits of society, along lines of greater equality than the mythical free market had seemingly produced. Changes in the tax code and laws dealing with wages and hours, social security, medical care for the aged, aid to depressed geographic areas, public housing, aid to inner-city public education, and job training all involve debates over equality or inequality and degrees of redistributiveness.

In its lawmaking function in the domestic realm, Congress is unlikely to surrender willingly any of the activities in which it is already involved. It certainly could, however, show some aggressiveness in seeking out new areas of endeavor, or it could deliberately seek simply to maintain the status quo in terms of the range of citizen activities in which it is involved.

Parenthetically, it should be added that this view of con-

167

gressional importance in various realms of public policy suggests that the classic statements about the executive branch gaining power at the expense of Congress are beside the point. If the total policy activity of the government is expanding, then increasing visibility for the executive relative to the visibility of Congress does not necessarily mean that Congress is therefore becoming less important. It may be playing a diminished policy role relative to the executive branch but an augmented absolute role in terms of the importance of its agenda to society. In short, legislative-executive relations are not profitably explored by continually seeking to answer the single question: "Who's on top?" [1]

In foreign affairs Congress has, especially in recent years, usually been peripheral and reluctant to assert itself. Whether this posture of Congress toward this part of its lawmaking authority will continue or not seems open to at least some question. Will Congress again pass a Tonkin Gulf type of resolution, for example? (There have been a number of such resolutions passed since World War II involving not just Southeast Asia but also involving Western Europe, the Mideast, and the Far East.) Or will a president even feel confident enough to ask for such a resolution? It is no doubt true that Congress cannot absolutely control foreign affairs and probably should not do so. It is also true that Congress can show varying degrees of assertiveness or unassertiveness in dealing with such problems.

Another important element of variance that can occur in congressional performance of the lawmaking function is the degree of specificity in the standards of administering various laws that are included in the organic statutes themselves. Congress can decide about the level of specificity in many different

[1] Richard Neustadt has made the interesting suggestion that the really important "who's on top" question should not pit the executive against Congress but rather should pit the politicians in Congress and the executive on the one hand against the career bureaucrats in the executive on the other. The pattern of Vietnam involvement may well provide fascinating and frightening evidence to substantiate Neustadt's view. See Richard E. Neustadt, "Politicians and Bureaucrats," in David B. Truman, ed., *The Congress and America's Future* (Englewood Cliffs, N.J.: Prentice-Hall, 1965).

ways. At one extreme, for example, the Social Security Act of 1935 contains remarkably clear standards to guide subsequent administration of the law. At the other extreme, the phrase "maximum feasible participation" (of the poor) in the Economic Opportunity Act of 1964 meant many different things to federal administrators, city officials, and actual or potential beneficiaries.

CONGRESS AND OVERSIGHT OF ADMINISTRATION

Congress can oversee administrative activities in a variety of moods. It can pursue very narrow questions, such as "What did you do with the $10,000 for new downspouts at Fort Sill?" It can also pursue very broad questions, such as "What should the role of the federal government be in relation to the development of the nation's urban areas?". Much oversight approaches the Fort Sill end of the spectrum. Some members of Congress seem intent on becoming day-to-day managers of specific programs (some would, for example, charge that Congresswoman Edith Green of Oregon has been, at various times in her career, interested in running programs in juvenile delinquency or education rather than overseeing them.) However, a good deal of the other kind of oversight also takes place. In recent years the Ribicoff hearings on the federal government and the cities, the Clark hearings on manpower, the Jackson hearings on national-security organization, and the McGovern hearings on hunger, all qualify as policy oversight of administration of the broadest kind—concerned not just with administrative details but concerned with the scope and direction of policy in large and important areas.

CONGRESS AND EDUCATION OF THE PUBLIC

Congress as an institution has never devised an appropriate mode of communicating with the public.[2] Perhaps this is inevitable. As a multiheaded institution of equals with differing party affiliations and policy views it is hard to imagine Congress

[2] The House of Representatives established, for a while, an Office of the Coordinator of Information. It served no useful purpose, however, and was abandoned.

ever appearing as a single-minded entity to the public. There is no single spokesman for Congress, even on relatively non-controversial issues. Certainly the president has a natural advantage if he and a majority of Congress disagree over something fundamental. He can state his position clearly in public (with immediate and thorough coverage by the mass media) and the leaders of the majority view in Congress can try to counteract it. But the congressional posture is almost always muddied because there will also be a vocal minority in Congress supporting the presidential position publicly.

However, individual members of Congress certainly can and do engage in public education. Again, any given senator or representative can take a variety of stances. At one extreme stand those members who only try to gauge what is popular at any given time and assure themselves (they hope) of continued electoral success by following the voice of the people. At the other extreme stand those who try to lead their constituents, sometimes in directions they know to be unpopular.

CONGRESS AND REPRESENTATION

Congress is representative in many senses, and it has many interests it can represent—including interests as expressed by interest groups, but also including interests of constituencies, of territorial units such as cities, districts, states, or regions, and of the nation as a whole. Individual members of the House and Senate can and do undertake a number of different kinds of representative activities:

1. Members of the House and Senate support the interests of individuals in a variety of "casework" activities. These cases typically involve deportation and immigration, selective service, social security, and tax matters.

2. Members of the House and Senate also pursue cases involving corporate entities. Typically these cases will involve enforcement and interpretation of the tax code or exemptions from certain kinds of enforcement of regulatory provisions. For example, when strict application of federal safety standards threatened the last steamboat on the Ohio River with extinction, interested members of Congress from the region were successful in getting different standards applied to this particu-

lar boat. Defense contractors involved in cost-overrun disputes with the government can regularly count on some congressional intervention on their behalf.

3. Members of the House and Senate are also concerned with intervening in the division of federal largesse. Here they pursue such things as new post offices and dams for given localities and contracts for given companies.

4. Senators and representatives can also seek to represent broad classes or races. Some black members consider themselves representatives of the interests of all blacks; some conservative, white southerners consider themselves representatives of the interests of all southern whites and perhaps all whites. Some members consider themselves spokesmen for all the poor or for some segment of the poor—perhaps urban, perhaps Appalachian, perhaps Indian.

5. Finally, senators and representatives can choose to try to represent the national good. Presumably most of them take this stance at least some of the time. In this vein some members are even led to take stands that are unpopular and may cost them their seats. The early opposition of Senators Morse and Gruening to the war in Vietnam provides a case in point.

Most members of Congress, in fact, pursue a mixture of the above representative activities, although different members certainly weight the activities differently. Thus, it is not at all unusual to see a Senator like Morse vigorous in his antiwar stance on one day and vigorous in support of high tariffs to protect Oregon cherries the next. Nor is it unusual to see Senator Fulbright simultaneously pursuing national-interest concerns and a vigorous interest in the welfare of Arkansas chicken and rice growers.

Decision Making on Policy Questions by Individual Senators and Representatives

Figure 8–1 portrays, in highly simplified fashion, the pressures involved in the decision process by which an individual senator or representative makes up his mind on what position to take on any specific policy.

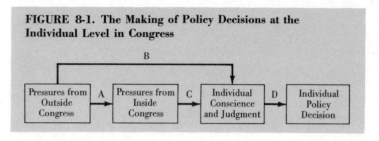

FIGURE 8-1. The Making of Policy Decisions at the Individual Level in Congress

In this figure, pressures from outside congress include those stemming from the public (mass opinion, the opinion of various specialized publics, and the opinion of voters as registered in their electoral decisions), interest groups, the various parts of the executive branch (the presidency and bureaucracies), and state and local officials. These pressures have an impact on the institutional clusters within Congress (relationship A in the figure) and also have an impact on the individual member directly (relationship B).

Pressures from inside Congress include those generated by party leaders, committee delegations, state delegations, informal clubs and groups, and staff members. These pressures impinge on the individual senator and representative (Relationship C). (It should also be noted that these various sources of outside and inside pressure also have a vast array of interrelations among themselves.)

Once the individual has received the various outside and inside pressures, he views them through the filters of his conscience and judgment and reaches his decision on his position and on his behavior (his position and his behavior usually coincide).

Political Parties and Congress

Political parties are the key link between Congress and both the outside world (in the form of voters) and the overall policy and program wishes of the president. The parties that are most important in this linkage function are congressional parties.

Once a candidate for Congress has been elected and reaches his destination in the House or Senate, he is confronted with the congressional party. This party possesses machinery that is likely to have a much greater impact on him than will either the national party (under whose banner he ran for office) or the state and local parties (whose organization may have helped him as he campaigned). The leaders, caucuses, party committees, and other features of the congressional party impinge on his daily life and are responsible for such crucial items in his congressional career as committee assignments. They control the business on the floor, and he must come to some terms with his party if he is to hope for success in pushing bills and policies that he favors through Congress. In short, the parties in Congress provide absolutely essential procedural controls over the business of Congress. Centrally, they provide order and efficiency in the legislative process.

The congressional parties also possess some substantive content. Until the twentieth century the congressional parties generated their own substantive positions, but attention was narrowly focused, mainly on changing tariffs and perhaps one or two other areas during the course of a congress.

In the twentieth century the leaders of the party of the president typically (and undeviatingly since 1933) have accepted most of his policies and program preferences as their own. The leaders of the president's party in the House and Senate usually work for the success of these preferences without seriously questioning them or balking at supporting them. The president's preferences are generally consistent with the national-party platform although rarely identical with it. His legislative program is, of course, much more than a personal program. It is developed by the entire bureaucracy under the guidance of the Office of Management and Budget and other parts of the institutional presidency.

As the president's program comes to the committees and the floor in each house of Congress, most of the members of his party support most of it. There may be considerable dissent over portions of his program, but the common party label shared with the president helps motivate most members to avoid dissent when possible. Party label is both a symbol and a reality that provides a focus for loyal behavior on substantive issues. Shared experiences, friendships, and party machinery all help reinforce the natural feelings of loyalty to the president and his program in the members of his party.

The party without a president in the White House has a more difficult time in generating loyalty to a substantive program. This party can decide to oppose the president and his party in a variety of ways (with or without alternatives), or it can partially support the program or try to participate in the development of some of it (an exceedingly difficult task). Typically, the opposition party has even less of a programmatic or substantive identity than the presidential party.

In addition to the relation between congressional parties and substantive content, congressional parties are also interesting from another aspect, namely that party affiliation is a better predictor of votes on the floor of the House and Senate than any other factor. A recent study of voting in Congress from 1921 through 1964 concluded that "by any measure party remains the single most important factor in roll call voting."[3] The trend during this time period was toward weaker party unity on controversial issues, principally because of the growing ideological conservatism on the part of a number of southern Democrats. Nevertheless, party remained a relatively strong uniting force in Congress.

Party Leadership in Congress

Party leaders in Congress provide the order and procedural stability that allows Congress to produce a large quantity of policy statements and actions.

Throughout history there have been a great variety of patterns of leadership used by both parties in both the House and the Senate. Little has been static in the specific arrangements for institutional leadership that have evolved. There has, how-

[3] Julius Turner, *Party and Constituency: Pressure on Congress*, rev. ed., Edward V. Schneier, Jr., ed. (Baltimore: Johns Hopkins, 1970).

ever, been stability in the sense that since roughly the 1880s the formal leaders of both parties in both houses have been extremely important in helping to determine what finally emerges from the House and the Senate.

The following sections deal with the present leadership in the House and the Senate (a leadership that has been relatively stable since the early 1960s in terms of institutional arrangements and the styles of the principal leaders—even though some of the individuals have changed).

THE LEADERSHIP PATTERNS

The *House Democrats* in the 1960s and early 1970s had a leadership pattern in which a three-man group (the Speaker, the majority leader, and the majority whip) formed the core. This group met daily to plan the general strategy and the specific tactics of action on the House floor. As specific bills were reported as ready for floor consideration by the various House committees, the three-man group would co-opt a committee leader, usually the chairman, to work with them on tactical details of passing the committee's bill.

To aid the core group the House Democrats also had a whip organization consisting of a deputy whip and eighteen regional whips in addition to the chief whip. The Committee on Committees for the party, although not totally dominated by the core group, helped perform the leadership function of assigning Democrats to standing committees. This group consisted of the Democratic members of the Ways and Means Committee, with each member specially responsible for a state or regional cluster of states. In 1973 the speaker, majority leader, and caucus chairman were added as voting members. In addition, all Democrats meeting together in the caucus also helped perform some leadership functions.

The *House Republicans* had a more diffused pattern of leadership during the 1960s and early 1970s. At least five positions carried leadership status in the Republican party (although it was much smaller than the Democratic party in the House): the minority leader, the chairman of the conference (the Republican version of the Democratic caucus), the minority whip, the chairman of the Policy Committee, and the chairman of the Research and Planning Committee. These leaders did not always meet together on a harmonious basis, because of the personality differences that cropped up during part of the period (particularly in the early 1960s).

The Republican leaders were also aided by a whip organization and by the members of the Policy Committee and the Research and Planning Committee. In addition the Republicans had a large committee on committees to perform the function of assigning Republicans to standing committees. As indicated below, this committee tended to be relatively independent of the principal individual leaders but it did perform a leadership function. The full Conference also helped with one of the leadership functions.

In addition, the norms and traditions of the Republican party in the House also gave unusually heavy weight to the senior Republican members of various standing committee delegations. (Senior Democrats on standing committees were also important in their party but not as independent within their party as the senior Republicans within theirs.)

The *Senate Democrats* operate with a minimum of centralized leadership. The only consistently important individual in a Senate leadership position is the majority leader. During the entire 1960s and early 1970s the majority leader has been Mike Mansfield (D-Montana), an individual with a low-key approach to the task of leading. In theory he is aided by a majority whip and the secretary of the party conference (the total Democratic membership). There are also four deputy whips, a steering committee, and a policy committee. However, the majority whip, secretary, and deputy whips perform mainly housekeeping chores; the majority leader himself chairs the Steering Committee and the Policy Committee. He is certainly constrained by the deliberations in those committees, but if he chooses he can also be the important figure in those deliberations. Although Mansfield did not choose to be dominant most of the time, the potential in the position clearly exists (as was well-illustrated by Mansfield's predecessor in the 1950s, Lyndon B. Johnson of Texas).

The *Senate Republicans* limit the activities of the minority leader with committees not chaired by him. Nevertheless, the minority leader is the single most important figure in the party. He is aided by a minority whip, the chairman of the conference, and the chairman and members of the Policy Committee. The Senate Republicans also have a committee on committees with a separate chairman but, as will be explained below, this committee does not have much to do independently of an automatic rule of seniority for making committee assignments.

THE LEADERSHIP FUNCTIONS

The leaders of all four congressional parties perform (or at least have the potential of performing) five major functions.

First, the leaders help organize the party to conduct business. Essentially this means that they participate in the selection of new leaders and the decisions concerning who will sit on which committees. The choice of leaders and committee members is, of course, a choice that determines which individuals with which set of beliefs will be sitting in the most critical institutional positions when policy decisions are made.

In the House Democratic party the caucus elects the Speaker, the majority leader, and the members of the Ways and Means Committee. Usually, the Speaker can determine who the majority leader will be if he announces his preference publicly or lets it be widely known privately, although some Speakers have refrained from making their choice known. The Speaker can also usually endorse winning candidates for the Ways and Means vacancies, although occasionally the caucus will choose someone other than the Speaker's candidate. The Speaker and the majority leader appoint the whip. The Speaker and the majority leader can also have an influence on committee assignments made by the Committee on Committees. This influence is used selectively, but it means that in at least a few policy areas the leaders can help predetermine policy statements and actions emanating from a specific committee by helping see to it that the membership is predisposed to certain kinds of policy positions congenial to the leaders. For example, in the 1950s Speaker Sam Rayburn transformed the House Education and Labor Committee from a conservative body to a more liberal one by personally superintending new Democratic appointments.

In the House Republican party the conference elects minority leader, the minority whip, and the chairman of the conference. The committee on committees is constituted entirely through the state delegations—with one member of the committee coming from every state that has at least one Republican in the House. In this party the minority leader (and the other central leaders, too) have minimal influence on the choice of other leaders and on the decisions of the committee on committees.

In both Senate parties the leadership seems disposed not to play a very active role in helping with the leader and committee choices in the party. Every individual senator seems to be fending for himself, and little central direction is evident in organizational terms in either party.

Second, the leaders—particularly of the majority party—are responsible for scheduling the business to come to the House and the Senate floors. In the House, the Speaker and majority leader make these decisions, although they occasionally consult the minority leader to make sure that his sense of fairness is not violated. In the Senate the majority leader routinely consults the minority leader; if they agree they have great flexibility because the Senate usually proceeds in ad hoc fashion under so-called unanimous consent agreements. Naturally, the scheduling decisions made in both houses are not neutral but can be used to influence the chances of success or failure of specific pieces of legislation.

Third, the leaders are responsible for promoting attendance on the floor of the House and the Senate. Both of the parties in the House do this primarily through their whip organizations, which are responsible for being able to locate and contact all party members within a short period of time to tell them that a critical vote is at hand and their presence is required. In the Senate, an individual senator who is interested in a piece of legislation will do his own "whipping" to increase attendance, because neither party's whip apparatus is used routinely.

Obviously, selectivity is exercised in the activity designed to increase attendance. For example, the whip organization of one of the House parties may well not contact a known opponent of the leaders' position when a critical vote is imminent.

Fourth, the leaders are all engaged in the constant collection and distribution of information. Reliable information is a precious commodity in both houses. In the House the whip organizations in both parties serve as focal points for the performance of the information function. Members' attitudes on selected upcoming bills are solicited, and the leaders in turn disseminate to their party members information on their preferences and limited information on the content of proposed legislation. In the Senate individual senators particularly interested in a bill usually wind up doing their own headcounts and their own distribution of substantive information.

Fifth, the leaders of both parties in both houses are involved in maintaining liaison with the White House on policy matters. This involves those leaders of the president's party more frequently than the leaders of the other party. Usually the leaders of the president's party meet with him weekly as a matter of routine. There may be other meetings, and the members of the opposition party may also be invited from time to time for specific briefings and consultation. Presumably the leaders can serve as mediators between the president and the rank-and-file members, helping to facilitate the flow of policy-related information and preferences in both directions.

In short, all five of these functions are capable of being performed in such a way as to enhance the possibility of attaining specific, desired policy statements and actions and reducing the possibility of producing undesired statements and actions. The leaders' central task is to persuade members to support their policy preferences on the floor of the House and Senate. It should be noted, however, that the content of a leader's preferences are usually based upon the stance of his party's delegation in the relevant standing committee for any given issue. That is, the leaders usually take their substantive cues from a committee delegation and then exercise their persuasive powers to gain ratification for that position, rather than attempting to push a personal position on their party in an authoritarian manner.

THE PRINCIPAL LEADERSHIP RESOURCES FOR INFLUENCING POLICY RESPONSES

The party leaders in both houses have four principal resources at their disposal as they labor to influence the policy statements and actions emerging from the Senate and the House. They do not always use all of the resources at their disposal and different leaders have styles that vary greatly from relatively passive to quite active.

The first resource in the hands of the leaders is their ability to use the rules. This ability is formally given to them by the rules of the House and the Senate, and out of desire and necessity leaders develop considerable expertise in manipulating the intricacies of the rules.

In the House, the majority party leaders, particularly the Speaker, are in a very strong position to use the rules to further policy ends favored by the leaders. The minority leaders in the House have some obstructive powers but the House rules generally put the majority party in a consistently dominant position. For example, the Speaker has discretion in what he puts on the suspension calendar, a device for expediting relatively noncontroversial bills (bills brought to the floor on this calendar are debated for only forty minutes and require a two-thirds vote for passage). Many bills of low visibility would die if they were not moved through the House quickly in this fashion. This means that the Speaker is in a good position to build credits for the future or to reward past loyalty or to punish past disloyalty by either granting or withholding a member's request to place on the suspension calendar a bill that is important to him but that may die without expedition.

In the Senate the leaders of both parties have influence over the use of the rules. As previously indicated, the Senate is a flexible institution because of the device of unanimous consent agreements. The leaders play a central role in arranging these agreements, thereby enhancing their ability to collect IOUs for the future, as well as rewarding and depriving for the past.

The second resource possessed by the leaders is their control over a number of forms of tangible preferment. Tangible preferments include appointments to special and select committees, commissions, and delegations to foreign meetings; appointments to standing committees; help in pushing specific bills; and help aimed at reelection. Again the granting or withholding of such preferments is used selectively to enhance the odds that the leaders will get their way when they ask for specific policy actions.

The leaders of both houses have a great deal of control over appointments to special and select committees, commissions, and foreign delegations. This control over assignments to standing committees is less evident but can be significant. In the House, for example, the Democratic Committee on Committees will not appoint a Democrat to the Rules Committee without the approval of the Speaker. The Democratic leaders can also intervene selectively in the assignments to other committees. In the 1950s, Speaker Rayburn saw to it that the Democratic membership on the Education and Labor Committee was reoriented from conservative to reliably liberal. In general, the Democratic Committee on Committees pays some attention to party loyalty in making assignments, and those members more loyal to the party are more likely to receive their preferred assignments.[4]

The House Republican leaders have much less influence over standing committee assignments. The Committee on Committees is selected and operated so that, typically, a few senior conservatives from the states with the largest Republican delegations effectively make the decisions. This means that the Republican delegations on the most important committees are heavily weighted in the conservative direction.

In the Senate the leaders have only minor influence on committee assignments. This is particularly true in the Republican

[4] For empirical evidence on this point, see Randall B. Ripley, *Party Leaders in the House of Representatives* (Washington, D.C.: Brookings, 1967), pp. 59–61.

party, where the Committee on Committees make initial assignments on the basis of seniority (that is, if two individuals apply for the same opening, the more senior automatically gets it). The influence of the Republican leaders can be seen only occasionally, when they might ask a more senior person to apply for an opening in order to keep an undesirable senator off the committee. The Democratic Steering Committee (which is the committee on committees) is not bound by seniority and the majority leader chairs the committee. But his degree of influence is related to his degree of aggressiveness; Senator Mansfield is unaggressive about most aspects of his leadership role.

The leaders of all four parties can facilitate or impede committee and floor consideration of specific bills.

Campaign help can be channeled to particularly helpful members by the leaders. Both of the congressional Republican parties have several million dollars at their disposal to aid candidates (both incumbents and nonincumbents). This can be given on a selective basis, with maverick incumbents getting little or no aid. The Democratic congressional parties have much less money at their disposal, and so the impact of the aid is considerably reduced. The leaders of all four parties can personally campaign for a few incumbents each year. Obviously it is very flattering for a rank-and-file congressman to have the Speaker or the majority leader speak personally in his district during a campaign. These appearances are rare and are, like most scarce commodities, highly valued by those who benefit.

The third resource the leaders can use to affect policy statements and actions is their control over psychological preferment. This simply means that the leaders, particularly in the House, are in a position to give cues on how highly they value an individual member. These cues, once given, help establish a member's reputation. Since most House members are desirous of a career in the House and since they need the respect and good will of the leaders and their fellow members to make that career a successful one in terms of achievement of legislative goals, they are extremely sensitive to the leaders' cues.

Skillful leaders can help sway member behavior by the content and timing of the cues and by careful selection of the audience to receive them.

Senators also need respect and good will in the Senate if they are to be deemed successful legislators. On the other hand, senators can also command wider attention than that accorded them by their fellow members, and many may not worry excessively about their legislative effectiveness. They can also attain gratification by being a public figure in their state or region or even in the whole nation. Almost any senator can command good newspaper space in his state and with a little extra effort can be quoted and pictured regionally or nationally. This opportunity is not open to most House members, which means that they are very sensitive to their reputational standing in the House. Senators who are above all desirous of being good legislators (or having the reputation for quality in that area) are susceptible to psychological preferment manipulated by the leaders. Senator Mansfield has not been active in this vein, although his predecessor, Lyndon Johnson, was masterful at it.[5] The Republican leaders in the 1960s and 1970s were somewhere between Mansfield and Johnson in their level of activity.

The fourth resource that can be used by the leaders in seeking specific legislative action is their dominance over the communications process internal to the House and Senate. The leaders are in a unique position to influence what is learned about the schedule, the rules, and the intentions of the president, themselves, and other key members about pending legislation. Particularly in the House the members of both parties routinely look to their party leaders for reliable information on such matters (although they are not heavily dependent on their party leaders for information on the substance of legislation—for that they rely on the standing committee members from their party). Even in the Senate a skillful leader, like Johnson, can make the senators of his party (and even of the

---

[5] For a good discussion of Johnson as leader, see Rowland Evans and Robert Novak, *Lyndon B. Johnson: The Exercise of Power* (New York: New American Library, 1966).

other party) come to him or his staff members for the most current and most reliable information.

The dominance over the communications process means that the leaders sit in a critical location in relation to a variety of two-way communications. Thus, they learn as well as inform and can use their knowledge to enhance their chances for success by urging minor but critical amendments, for example, or by changing the schedule to accommodate a number of members who are in the leaders' camp on a given bill.

Congressional Committees and Public Policy

Most of the qualitative impact of Congress on policy statements and actions occurs in the standing committees of the House and Senate. The committees are only partially and sporadically subject to party and party-leader influence. They are highly susceptible to influence from the executive branch's bureaus, from interest groups, and from constituency and clientele groups.

Different committees in the House and the Senate behave very differently from one another. Some are dominated by the chairman acting alone; some are run by an oligarchy of the most senior members; others operate fairly democratically. Even in the more democratic committees, however, the chairman still can have a good deal of impact on policy statements and actions emerging from the committee unless he is completely inept for one reason or another.

Committees also vary greatly in their ideological perspective. Through the years some committees appear to develop a tradition of liberalism and new recruits tend to come from the ranks of liberals. Likewise, new recruits to committees with norms of conservatism tend to be conservatives to begin with or at least quite susceptible to a conservative socialization experience. Usually, committees change ideologies only gradually, barring a major electoral overturn or a major intervention in the committee assignment process by the party leaders.

Committees tend to make decisions by sampling the vast

range of information presented to them. This is particularly true of the appropriations subcommittees faced with mountains of detailed data but is also generally true of all committees.[6] Speaking specifically about the appropriations subcommittees Richard Fenno, a leading student of congressional committees, has said:

> Committee members sample for three kinds of information—*program* information, *confidence* information, and *support* information. They want to know about agency programs, of course, to see whether those programs accord with their view of the public interest and to see how effectively such programs are being carried out. Here, subcommittee members sample by focusing their attention on that part of the budget request which represents a change from the previous year's appropriation. . . .
> Perhaps the most consistent thread in subcommittee decision making is the sampling they do for the purpose of deciding whether or not to tender their confidence to an agency. . . .
> The third kind of information desired by subcommittee members pertains to the size, shape, and intensity of outside support for agency programs.[7]

There are several interrelated, general differences between committees in the House and committees in the Senate. In the Senate, on the one hand, virtually all Senators find great satisfaction in the present committee system, because of the opportunities it affords them for developing personal influence.[8]

They occasionally are ignored by the system but the annoyances are relatively minor. In the assignment process in both parties most individual senators can usually count on receiving at least one committee that interests them. Once on a committee they can usually find one or two congenial subcommittees

[6] See Richard F. Fenno, "The Impact of PPBS on the Congressional Appropriations Process," in Robert L. Chartrand, Kenneth Janda, and Michael Hugo, eds., *Information, Support, Program Budgeting, and the Congress* (New York: Spartan Books, 1968), pp. 175–194.

[7] *Ibid.*, pp. 181–182.

[8] For a fuller development of this point, see Randall B. Ripley, *Power in the Senate* (New York: St. Martin's, 1969).

that handle matters in which they can rapidly become expert. They soon make decisions within the subcommittee and committee either by themselves (with the aid of staff) or perhaps with the agreement of one senator from the other party. These decisions are almost automatically ratified on the floor. In short, although committee influence is not distributed equally, it is widely distributed, and most chairmen in the Senate are relatively comfortable presiding over a widespread dispersion of influence. This makes for highly decentralized decision making and, at the same time, well-pleased senators.

In the House, on the other hand, the committees are typically larger and more centralized. Many chairmen keep a tighter control over the proliferation of subcommittees than the typical Senate chairman, and many of the subcommittee chairmen themselves run relatively "tight ships" in which a large number of members attend but the more senior members dominate. Thus, the portion of the House membership sitting on such committees and subcommittees are not, at least in their junior years, particularly enamored of the committee system. Many junior members find themselves relatively unimportant in any policy area whatsoever.

There are at least three major factors related to committees that help to explain why the policy statements and actions emerging from different committees vary.[9] First, the goals of the members in seeking membership on a committee are important. Second, the specific environment within which the committee works has a decided impact. Third, the basic decision rules adopted (perhaps unknowingly) by the committee help predetermine the kinds of policy statements and actions in which the committee will engage. Table 8–1 summarizes the nature of these factors for six committees in the House. The policy statements and actions emerging from these six committees show the influence of member's goals, environmental constraints, and the basic decision rules.

The Appropriations Committee (in practice, its subcom-

[9] The following discussion is adapted from Richard F. Fenno, Jr., *Congressmen in Committees* (Boston: Little, Brown, 1973).

TABLE 8-1. Factors Related to Policy Responses for Six House Committees

			Committee			
	Appropriations	Ways and Means	Foreign Affairs	Education and Labor	Post Office and Civil Service	Interior and Insular Affairs
Members' Goals	Maximize influence in the House	Maximize influence in the House	Maximize influence in a given policy area	Maximize influence in a given policy area	Maximize chances of reelection to the House	Maximize chances of reelection to the House
Environmental Constraints	Parent chamber coalitions led by executive agencies	Parent chamber coalitions led by partisan clusters in the House and by executive agencies	Coalitions led by executive agencies (mainly State Department and AID)	Coalitions led by partisan groups in and out of the House	Coalitions led by clients (civil-service unions and 2nd- and 3rd-class mailers)	Coalitions led by clients (many and diverse)
Basic Decision Rules	1. Reduce executive budget requests 2. Provide adequate funding for executive programs	1. Write bills that will pass the House 2. Allocate credit to majority party for policies adopted	Approve and help pass the foreign-aid bill	1. Allocate credit to parties for policies adopted 2. Pursue individual policy preferences regardless of partisan implications	1. Support maximum pay increases and benefits for civil servants; and to oppose all postal-rate increases 2. Accede to executive-branch wishes if necessary to assure some pay and benefit increases	1. Secure House passage of all constituency-supported, member-sponsored bills 2. Balance the competing demands of conservationists and private users of land and water resources so as to give special benefits to users

Source: Adapted from Richard F. Fenno, Jr., *Congressmen in Committees* (Boston: Little, Brown, 1973).

mittees) generally cuts budgets proposed by the executive branch by almost a fixed percentage (rarely greater than ten percent and usually considerably lower), but the basic reliance is still on the executive request—the executive branch sets the agenda. Thus, the committee responds to the executive-led coalitions and follows its basic decision rules of reducing executive budget requests while still providing adequate funding for the programs administered by the executive branch. At the same time the power of the committee to cut at least some things selectively (and also the power to add some things selectively) does help the members realize their private goals of increasing their influence in the House.

The Ways and Means Committee passes carefully worked out versions of essentially majority-party positions on the range of subjects within the committee's jurisdiction (trade, social security, and taxation are the three major items). The craftsmanship that goes into the final versions is designed to insure that the final product will pass the House. But the majority-party stamp is also clearly on that product, so that when it passes the majority party can take most of the public credit for it (even though the minority party may have made a considerable contribution). The products coming from the committee show responsiveness to the partisan coalitions (especially that within the majority party) paying attention to the subject, and they also show responsiveness to the views of the Social Security Administration, the president, the treasury, and other parts of the executive branch working in these areas. However, the committee rarely simply passes an executive request without putting its own stamp on it.

The large amount of activity in which the Ways and Means Committee engages on issues within the House that are highly visible and that have important ramifications for constituents (trade, taxation, and social security/medicare all fit this description) means that subject matter alone will make the members visible and sought after by their colleagues. This enhances their influence. In addition, the Democratic members serve as members of the Democratic Committee on Committees and are, therefore, accorded additional influence. Thus, the committee procedures and policies allow members to realize their goal of enhancing their influence.

The Foreign Affairs Committee's major policy activities involve the annual foreign-aid authorization bill. Here the committee always approves the bill in a form acceptable to the executive branch. Minor cuts and changes are made, but the committee does not introduce major changes to the House floor. This product obviously shows the committee responding to the executive-led coalition and following its basic decision rule of approving and helping to pass the foreign-aid bill. To the extent that individual members go on the committee to help support foreign aid they perhaps can feel that they are maximizing their impact on this policy area, although that impact does not appear to be independent but rather dependent on the executive branch.

The Education and Labor Committee is in almost a constant state of partisan turmoil. Much of its policy activity consists of heated debates and arguments inside the committee over a whole range of controversial measures involving labor relations, the War on Poverty, and a variety of educational aid measures. When agreement is possible among a majority of the committee members (usually composed almost entirely of members of the majority party), then controversial measures are brought to the floor, although with no guarantee that they are in a form that can pass the House. If the measures reported by the committee pass, then certainly the majority party will get the bulk of the credit; that party is also running a fair risk that major controversial bills brought to the floor will not pass.

At the same time all members of the committee can pursue matters that interest them personally, because there is no norm within the committee that winning on the House floor is very important. Therefore, if teams and majorities emerge, that is fine, but if they do not, members can still pursue their own interests and have the feeling that they are maximizing their influence on policy areas that intrigue them. When a majority of the committee is able to agree on a major issue, then it is certainly being basically responsive to partisan groups within the committee and within the House.

The Post Office and Civil Service Committee increases the pay of federal civil servants rather steadily. First-class postage rates also increase fairly frequently. Commercial users of the mails (magazines and "junk" mailers) are more protected by the committee, and increases in their rates are more gradual. These policy activities by the committee reflect their basic decision rule of supporting pay raises. That postal rates also go up indicates that the executive branch basically demands such increases as part of the price for increasing pay rates; the committee accedes to at least some of these demands rather than jeopardizing the increased pay. Certainly the policy decisions made by the committee reflect their responsiveness to the civil-servant and postal-employee unions that are constantly pressing for higher wages and to the second-class and third-class mailers that are constantly pressing for continued government subsidy of their mailing privileges with rates below cost. The favors that committee members get to do for federal workers (and every district has lots of postmen and may have other major federal installations) does help them maximize their chances for reelection both because, in gratitude, they might earn votes and campaign contributions from the unions (or perhaps from second-class and third-class mailers). After 1970, however, the power of the committee declined because the newly-created U.S. Postal Service was given more autonomy than the Post Office Department had had.

The Interior and Insular Affairs Committee produces a mixture of legislation, some of it applauded by conservationists and offensive to the users of public resources (grazers, timbering interests, mining interests) and some of it favorable to the users and anathema to the conservationists. This mixed pattern of legislation reflects the conflicting pressures on the members of the committee, virtually all of whom come from western districts in which there are large numbers of users and increasing numbers of vocal conservationists. These cross-pressured members seeking to maximize reelection chances naturally seek to turn out a balanced product that will placate all of the interests partially and offend none of them totally.

190

Summary

Congress is basically a changing collection of individuals making a broad range of decisions through the exercise of its various policy-related functions. It is often portrayed as an unchanging body because, in fact, there are relatively stable groups and institutions (such as the political-party organizations and standing committees) within the two houses that change only gradually and seem to dominate both the procedural and substantive activities of Congress. Nevertheless, Congress is capable of changing with relative speed when conditions seem to demand such speed, and it is also capable of aggressive policy activity—both in relation to the executive branch and in relation to the magnitude of the problems coming from society that it faces.

An open question, of course, is whether Congress chooses to be aggressive in any given situation. Often, it seems content to let problems aggregate until a crisis is perceived. It also seems content much of the time to let the executive branch set the agenda of government and propose the solutions. But, as this chapter seeks to make clear, there is nothing inherent in Congress that produces a passive or nonaggressive stance. It is no doubt difficult to mobilize a multiheaded institution, but it has been done in the past, and nothing has happened to the institution to prevent it from being done in the future. In short, the important place of Congress in the American scheme of government is secure unless members of the House and Senate themselves choose to give away the influence and power over policy statements and actions that is clearly theirs if they choose to exercise it.

CHAPTER 9

The Federal Courts

The federal courts are policy-making bodies and should be considered as such. The myth that Congress and the president make policy and the courts only interpret law is inaccurate. In the interpretation and application of law the courts have a highly policy-relevant role to play, and they play it willingly and, at times, aggressively. Virtually all of the highly emotional issues of American politics have been subject to court pronouncements. These pronouncements sometimes appear to fan the flames of controversy; at times they signal a diminution in the virulence of the controversy. Through the years the courts have been heavily involved in controversies over race (first slavery and later integration and segregation), religion (the separation of church and state), treatment of criminals, treatment of political dissenters and dissent, pornography, reapportionment of districts for legislative bodies, and the extent of the economic power of the federal government.

On some of these issues the courts have clearly taken the

lead in reshaping the content of public debate and in reshaping the content of the policies themselves. Currently, this is true in all of the areas mentioned above. There are also court pronouncements that, in effect, are overruled by the other organs of society. For example, in 1857 the Supreme Court in effect gave its blessing to the institution of slavery and to its expansion. Society, through a civil war, decreed otherwise. In a series of decisions prior to 1937 the courts had ruled that the federal economic power was limited and that the federal government simply could not do certain things. Society, through the reelection of Franklin Roosevelt (who had the power to appoint judges), provided the personnel for the court to decree, in effect, that the federal power over the economy (through the constitutional grant of power over any matter involving interstate commerce) was virtually unlimited, at least by the courts.

Before looking at the federal courts in some detail, it should also be noted that the federal courts are not the only important courts in the United States. As one close student of the judiciary has put it:

Notwithstanding this sharp increase in policy-making by the national judiciary, it remains true that in terms of both qualitative and quantitative criteria, an even greater amount of policy is made by the fifty state judicial systems. The volume of decisions made by the state courts is many times greater than the output of the national courts, and it is the state judicial systems—not the national—which have the function of resolving most of the litigational problems that arise in the lives of most of the people in the United States. These problems include (but are by no means limited to) conflicts involving marriage, divorce, the custody of children and the mentally ill, and other legal aspects of domestic relations; petty and grand theft, embezzlement, assault, robbery, breaking and entry, homicide, rape, forgery, auto theft, disorderly conduct, and other common crimes and misdemeanors; real property, negotiable instruments, sales, torts, contracts, and other business relationships; vagrancy, inebriation, sexual deviance, gambling, narcotics, and other "morals" offenses; industrial accidents, workmen's compensation, motor vehicle accidents, and other kinds of personal injury and property

193

damage; and labor-management relations, corporate organization, competitive practices, and other aspects of business practice.[1]

Likewise, it should be remembered that courts are not the only agencies that perform judicial functions. Up to a certain point in the legal process the police also act, in effect, as judges. Likewise, a number of administrative agencies scattered throughout the bureaucracy make what amount to judicial decisions about rates, the rights of individuals to benefits, and other matters that also get into the courts. A 1972 Supreme Court decision illustrates the point of how various supposedly separate functions often get blurred in practice.[2] In this decision the Court ruled unconstitutional the practice of many small-town mayors (chief executives) serving as judges in traffic cases, because the town treasuries obviously benefitted from the fines.

The Nature and Organization of the Federal Court System

There are three levels of federal courts. At the top of the pyramid is the Supreme Court with nine justices. Next are the courts of appeals. There are eleven judicial circuits in the country. Each circuit has one court of appeals that has from three to fifteen judges; nationwide there are ninety-seven courts-of-appeals judges.

The third level of federal court system is the district courts. These are trial courts for matters over which the federal government has jurisdiction. There are eighty-nine district courts scattered among the fifty states and District of Columbia. Every state has at least one court, and a few of the larger states have as many as four. Each district court has from one to twenty-four judges (depending on workload in the district); there are 331 district judges in the eighty-nine districts.

[1] Glendon Schubert, *Judicial Policy-Making* (Glenview, Ill.: Scott, Foresman, 1965), pp. 53–54.

[2] *Ward* v. *The Village of Monroeville* (41 U.S. Law Week 4011).

In addition to the central court system there are also some specialized federal courts: the Court of Claims, the Court of Customs and Patent Appeals, the Customs Court, the Court of Military Appeals, the Tax Court, and various courts in the territories of the United States. There is also an Administrative Office of the United States Courts to handle a variety of administrative matters.

The range of matters that can come to the attention of the central court system (the district courts, courts of appeals, and Supreme Court) is large. All cases involving the constitution, laws passed by Congress, treaties to which the United States is a party, and admiralty or maritime matters can automatically be brought in federal courts, no matter who the parties in the case are. Any kind of case can be brought in federal courts if it involves any of the following parties: (1) the United States, (2) two or more states, (3) a state and citizens of another state, (4) citizens of different states in disputes involving more than 10,000 dollars, (5) a state or citizens of a state and foreign nations or individuals, and (6) diplomatic representatives of foreign nations.

The federal courts do not make policy except through rulings in cases in which there are real adversaries who have something at stake in a real controversy, but sometimes the pronouncements in such cases have wide-ranging implications for policy or for the whole political system. Federal courts cannot take the initiative in seeking cases involving matters that they logically could consider. They have to wait for parties to bring cases to them in proper legal procedure. Therefore, some matters may go undecided for a long period of time until the legal process is engaged and a conclusion is worked out.

Most federal cases begin in a federal district court. There is a right of appeal to a court of appeals. Most cases end either in the district court or in a circuit court.

Table 9–1 summarizes the case loads of the three levels of federal courts in 1960 and 1970. The growth in work load in the decade of the 1960s is substantial.

The growing work load of district courts and courts of appeal has been handled in part by increasing the number of

195

TABLE 9-1. Case Loads of Principal Federal Courts, 1960 and 1970

| | 1960 | | 1970 | |
Type of Court	Cases Filed	Cases Terminated	Cases Filed	Cases Terminated
District Courts	89,112	91,693	127,280	117,254
Courts of Appeal	3,899	3,713	11,662	10,699
Supreme Court[a]	1,862	1,787	3,405	3,379

Source: Compiled from *Annual Report of the Director of the Administrative Office of the United States Courts* (1970), pp. 96, 106, 204; (1969), p. 180.

[a]October terms of 1959 and 1969 are used here.

judges. The Supreme Court, however, has had to cope with its increasing work load with essentially existing personnel (both judges and clerks). In late 1972 a study group appointed by the Chief Justice proposed a new National Court of Appeals to screen requests made to the Supreme Court for review of cases decided in lower courts and to decide finally some cases in which two different courts of appeals had reached different conclusions. The proposal immediately generated considerable controversy, and its fate is far from clear.

The Supreme Court can be very selective about the cases it hears. Two kinds of cases—those involving a state as a party and those involving a foreign diplomatic representative—can begin in the Supreme Court, although the court has considerable leeway in determining which cases it will actually accept. The rest of the Court's docket consists of cases on appeal. Some of these can come from state supreme courts in cases in which a claim of federal unconstitutionality for a state law is involved or in which the state court holds a federal law or treaty invalid. Most of the cases come through a device called a writ of certiorari, a procedure by which four of the nine justices must agree that a case is important enough to be considered by the Supreme Court. The Court grants only about one-eighth of the petitions for a writ of certiorari from the losing parties in cases in lower courts. Table 9–2 summarizes how the Supreme Court disposed of its cases during its 1959–60 and 1969–70 sessions. The Court reviews only a small proportion of the cases filed on the merits, and written opinions are relatively rare. Thus, when the Court does speak in a written opinion, it is safe to assume that it considers the matter an important one.

The Constitution gives Congress the power to create (or disband) courts other than the Supreme Court and also gives Congress the power to regulate the appellate jurisdiction of the Supreme Court. The latter power has been used only rarely despite periods in which a number of the members of Congress have been very hostile to lines of decision being made by the Court.

Although the Court itself is embedded in the Constitution, the size of its membership is not. The number of justices varied throughout its early history but has been stable at nine since 1869. President Franklin Roosevelt became extremely unhappy with Court decisions invalidating major parts of his New Deal program, and he moved dramatically in 1937 to have Congress

TABLE 9-2. Method of Disposition of Cases by the Supreme Court, 1960 and 1970[a]

	1960	1970
Total Cases Disposed during Term	1,787	3,379
Total Cases Disposed on the Merits	249	378
(By Written Opinion)	(110)	(105)
Total Cases Disposed of without Full Review on the Merits	1,538	3,001

Source: Adapted from *Annual Report of the Director of the Administrative Office of the United States Courts* (1970), p. 209; (1969), p. 183.

a. Data include the October terms of 1959 and 1969.

expand the Court to fifteen members. Congress declined to do so but only after a long public debate that helped convince a few sitting members of the Court that they had better be more flexible in approving (or at least in not disapproving) the economic initiatives of the rest of the government.

The major policy impact of the courts comes through the constitutional decisions they make, particularly those made by the Supreme Court. The lines of decision tend to change slowly because courts and the legal system generally are devoted to the binding nature of precedent. Occasionally, however, courts will simply flatly overrule their earlier decisions. The most dramatic example in recent times was the 1954 Supreme Court decision specifically declaring that segregated education was by nature a violation of the clause of the Fourteenth Amendment to the constitution guaranteeing the "equal protection of the laws" to all citizens. This specifically overruled an 1896 decision that had said that separate segregated public schools were constitutional as long as they were equal. However, even in this case the court had been moving toward such a decision for about a decade in other cases dealing with public-supported graduate and professional education.

Courts, Political Parties, and Geography

The federal court system is tied directly to party politics and to geographical political differences. Despite the theoretical supremacy of Supreme Court decisions over the behavior of district and appeals courts, the actual policies pursued in some major areas vary by the region in which the courts sit. Decisions also vary with the political party of the district or circuit judges involved.

THE IMPACT OF PARTY

The president appoints all federal judges and the Senate confirms these appointments. All of the appointments involve partisan considerations. The district- and special-court judgeships are particularly political, and partisan figures are usually nominated by local party officials (almost completely from the party of the president). Almost all elevations of district judges to courts of appeals seats (and that is the most normal source of recruitment for appellate judges) are judges of the president's party—again senators and representatives and local officials and leaders of the president's party have a major voice in making the decisions. Appointments to the Supreme Court are also highly partisan. Since World War II, for example, the president has only named two justices from a party other than his own.

Table 9–3 summarizes appointments to federal judgeships other than Supreme Court seats from 1884 through 1970. There is some variation but basically all presidents appear as highly partisan.

TABLE 9-3. Relevance of Party in Lower-Court Appointments, 1884-1970

President	Percentage of Judicial Appointments from Party of President
Cleveland	100.0% (N = 37)
Harrison	89.7% (N = 29)
McKinley	95.7% (N = 23)
T. Roosevelt	97.2% (N = 72)
Taft	82.2% (N = 35)
Wilson	98.6% (N = 72)
Harding	97.3% (N = 44)
Coolidge	94.1% (N = 68)
Hoover	85.7% (N = 49)
F. Roosevelt	95.9% (N = 194)
Truman	92.8% (N = 125)
Eisenhower	94.8% (N = 174)
Kennedy	91.0% (N = 122)
Johnson	94.6% (N = 168)
Nixon (1969-70)	96.6% (N = 89)

Source: Figures for Cleveland through Eisenhower appear in Richard J. Richardson and Kenneth N. Vines, *The Politics of Federal Courts* (Boston: Little, Brown, 1970), p. 68. Reprinted with permission from Little, Brown. The figures for Kennedy through Nixon were calculated from data in Congressional Quarterly's *Guide to the Congress of the United States* (Washington, D.C.: Congressional Quarterly, 1971), p. 237.

These partisan affiliations make a difference. For example, analysis has shown that on labor relations issues Democratic judges are predictably more prolabor than Republican judges. An civil-liberties issues Republican judges are predictably more civil libertarian than Democratic judges.[3]

THE IMPACT OF GEOGRAPHY

Federal judges are products of the districts and regions in which they serve. Most federal district courts have judges who grew up and acquired legal and political notice in the district. Courts of appeals are basically staffed with individuals from the regions for which the courts are responsible.

That regional variations in the homes of judges make a difference is dramatically illustrated in Figure 9–1. This figure relates decisions in cases involving blacks in southern district courts to the percentage of the black population in those districts. In general, the relationship holds that the higher the black population in the district, the lower the proportion of cases decided in favor of blacks in cases involving race relations. This parallels a well-known southern political phenomenon: the most conservative areas politically are those with the highest black populations (with a few urban exceptions like Atlanta), and the more liberal areas are those with relatively few blacks in the population.

The Courts and Their Publics

The federal court system has a number of publics or constituencies that constrain the decisions emerging from the system. The word *constituency* is usually used in connection with elected officials. Federal justices and judges are not, of course, elected. Nevertheless, the mass public does pay attention to the most visible of Supreme Court decisions and a variety of specialized publics (lawyers, state and local judges,

[3] Richard J. Richardson and Kenneth N. Vines, *The Politics of Federal Courts* (Boston: Little, Brown, 1970), p. 105.

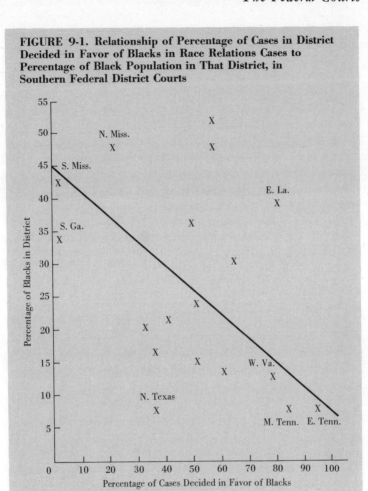

FIGURE 9-1. Relationship of Percentage of Cases in District Decided in Favor of Blacks in Race Relations Cases to Percentage of Black Population in That District, in Southern Federal District Courts

Source: Adapted from Richard J. Richardson and Kenneth N. Vines, *The Politics of Federal Courts* (Boston. Little, Brown, 1970), p. 97. Reprinted with permission from Little, Brown.

other federal officials in the executive and legislative branches, and state executive and legislative officials) also pay very close attention to what the Court is doing. Both the mass public and the specialized publics react to visible Supreme Court decisions.

Given the heavy involvement of the court system, particularly the Supreme Court, in politics and given the partisan nature of appointments, the Court almost invariably reflects major political trends in the country. However, because federal justices and judges are appointed for life, there is also inevitably an imperfect fit between the presence of a political or ideological trend in the nation and the reflection of that trend in the decisions of the Supreme Court. Thus, for example, the conservative ideology of the Court on economic questions, which was a faithful reflection of elections and majority opinion in the 1920s, continued to dominate the opinions of the Court until the middle to late 1930s, because the men appointed in the 1920s (and, in some cases, earlier) continued to serve. Only well into his second term as president did Franklin Roosevelt have the opportunity to appoint men reflecting his views. These men in turn continued to serve throughout the 1950s and 1960s even though the political climate had become considerably more conservative, particularly on civil-rights and civil-liberties questions. In the early 1970s four vacancies on the Court occurred quickly, and so President Nixon moved to make his mark on the Court's philosophy on social issues, specifically announcing that he would appoint only "strict constructionists," that is, individuals who were unwilling to interpret constitutional mandates of governmental authority broadly. A distinctive Nixon court seems to be emerging.

It should be noted, of course, that trends of judicial decision do not change overnight, even with changes in personnel. The weight of precedent is great. For example, shortly after two of President Nixon's new appointees took their seats on the Supreme Court, the Court decided unanimously, in effect, to reject the president's position on slowing down public-school desegregation in the South. Several factors were probably at work here: both the momentum of earlier court decisions—that is, precedent—and the fact that nominee's positions on issues are not always fully predictable by the appointing president.

Thus, courts are somewhat insulated from day-to-day political trends, but if strong trends develop that alter the complexion of the White House and Congress, then the complexion of the Supreme Court (and also the lower courts) will inevitably be altered in the same way, albeit at a later period.

The popular hostility to the Court perceived by President Nixon and capitalized on in his 1968 campaign is present, or at least it was in the 1960s when the Court took a variety of liberal stances. Table 9–4 summarizes public response from 1966 to 1969 to the question asked by Gallup polling organization, "In general, what kind of rating would you give the Supreme Court—excellent, good, fair, or poor?" This table shows that overall the trend has been toward declining positive public evaluation and increasing negative public evaluation.

Table 9–5 summarizes 1969 data that suggests that the greatest hostility to (and least support for) the Court came from older persons, those with less education, and those living in the South. It also shows, however, that disenchantment with the Court was widespread throughout all age groups, educational categories, and regions.

The public is selective about what it does and does not like about the Court's policy performance. A poll conducted in 1966 by Louis Harris and his associates for the *Washington Post* asked respondents whether they approved or disapproved of six specific decisions made by the high court during the 1950s and 1960s.[4] The poll revealed that desegregation of schools and public accommodations was approved by about a two to one ratio, despite southern resistance. Also, despite vocal re-

TABLE 9-4. Public Rating of the Supreme Court, 1966-69

	1966	1967	1968	1969
Good or Excellent	43%	45%	36%	33%
Fair or Poor	41%	46%	53%	54%

Source: *Gallup Opinion Index*, vol. 49 (July, 1969), p. 14.

[4] This poll appears in G. Theodore Mitau, *Decade of Decision* (New York: Scribner's, 1967), p. 7.

TABLE 9-5. Public Rating of the Supreme Court, 1969, by Educational, Age, and Regional Categories

	Good or Excellent	Fair or Poor
Educational Level		
College	43%	52%
High School	32%	57%
Grade School	25%	51%
Age		
21–29	46%	44%
30–49	35%	54%
50 and Older	24%	59%
Region		
East	37%	51%
Midwest	33%	55%
South	24%	59%
West	34%	52%

Source: Adapted from *Gallup Opinion Index*, vol. 49 (July, 1969), p. 14.

sistance, the Court's position on reapportionment—insisting on equal numbers of people in all districts for the U.S. House of Representatives and for both houses of state legislatures—was approved by a three to one ratio. The split was fairly even on the wisdom of allowing Communists to have U.S. passports, and disapproval was strong on the decision to disallow confessions obtained without the presence of a lawyer for the accused (about a two to one ratio opposed) and on the decision outlawing the use of prayer in public schools (opposed by more than two to one).

The public also has opinions on what the philosophical complexion of the court should be. Table 9–6 shows that the overall break is about two to one in favor of appointing politically conservative individuals to the Court rather than politically liberal individuals. There has been very little change in this pattern of opinion since 1968.

Public opinion gets fed into the judicial decision-making process through politics. If a president sees political points to

TABLE 9-6. Opinion on Supreme Court Appointments[a]

	April, 1970	June, 1969	June, 1968
Liberal	27%	25%	30%
Conservative	49%	52%	51%
No Opinion	24%	23%	19%

Source: *Gallup Opinion Index*, vol. 49 (July, 1969), p. 15, and vol. 59 (May, 1970), p. 10.

a. The question asked was "When new appointments are made by the president to the Supreme Court, would you like to have these be people who are liberal or conservative in their political views?"

be gained by opposing or supporting some specific lines of decision, and if vacancies on the bench occur, he has the opportunity to appoint men to the Court who share his policy views and who will work, within the limits of precedent and incremental change, to support the positions that he has found to be politically popular. This source of input is, of course, one that requires time before results can be observed in the form of decisions from the Court compatible to the president's positions. And as mentioned earlier, the president has no assurance that the men he appoints to the Court will indeed echo his views in every decision they make; they certainly are under no legal or moral requirements to do so.

The Supreme Court and Public Policy

THE INCREMENTAL NATURE OF POLICY CHANGE

The point has already been made that the court system, led by the Supreme Court, changes its collective mind slowly. Overturns of constitutional decisions do not come overnight. Rather, modifications are made in existing precedent—sometimes in a more conservative direction and sometimes in a more liberal direction. Also, it should be noted that the terms *liberal* and *conservative* themselves are much too simple to cover many Supreme Court decisions. The law often requires complex reasoning, and the varieties of such reasoning that can take place often lead to a high degree of unpredictability about how individual justices will behave in any given case.

A good example of slow change involves the whole area of the rights of accused criminals.[5] In the 1950s and 1960s the "Warren Court" (named after former Chief Justice Earl Warren) greatly expanded the rights of accused criminals. Richard Nixon campaigned against the Warren Court in 1968, in part on the basis of these decisions. He asserted that society's rights were being ignored in the drive to protect the rights of the accused (including a large number who were guilty). He promised to make appointments to the Court that would help redress the balance between collective rights and individual rights. His first two appointments, Chief Justice Warren Burger and Justice Harry Blackmun, were in keeping with his promises, and by the end of the 1970–71 term of the court some changes had come about in the court's view of criminal rights. The specific changes make two points: first, that in a closely divided court (and many of the landmark decisions of the Warren Court in the criminal rights field had been made by 6–3 and 5–4 decisions) a few appointments can make a difference, and second, that even though the dominant philosophy of the members of the Court may change considerably, the change in policy statements as evidenced in decisions will proceed slowly and incrementally.

A specific example from 1970 makes both points. The controversial ruling of the Court in 1966 in *Miranda* v. *Arizona* that statements made by a defendant not warned of his constitutional rights were inadmissible as evidence against him in court, was narrowly decided, 5–4.[6] In 1971, in *Harris* v. *New York*, the reconstituted Court (now with two Nixon appointees) did not specifically overturn the earlier decision, but it did cut back on the scope of its application.[7] It sustained the

[5] The following discussion is based on an excellent analysis contained in *Congressional Quarterly Weekly Report* (Washington, D.C.: Congressional Quarterly, June 25, 1971), pp. 1390–1393.

[6] *Miranda* v. *Arizona* (384 U.S. 436).

[7] *Harris* v. *New York* (401 U.S. 222).

essence of the earlier decision that statements made by a defendant not warned of his constitutional rights were inadmissible as evidence against him, but it ruled that such statements, if voluntarily made, could be used against him to impeach his credibility if during his testimony in a trial he should contradict his earlier statement. Thus, it is clear that a change in the Court's composition can affect previous narrowly sustained decisions and that changes in decisions are made incrementally rather than abruptly.

In summing up the changed stance of the Court, *Congressional Quarterly* made the following observation: "Analysis of the *Harris* decision and others made during the years 1969–71 concerning issues of criminal law revealed a more conservative and restrained approach to questions of criminal rights, a tendency to limit—not expand—the Warren Court's landmark rulings but no sharp turn reversing these decisions.[8] In short, the Court could be seen in the period between 1969 and 1971 shifting to a posture of restraint and away from a posture of activism in the area of accused-criminals' rights.

ACTIVISM AND RESTRAINT IN JUDICIAL REVIEW

Judicial review simply means that the Supreme Court (and other courts, as well) can, in the course of considering specific cases, review both laws and the acts of officials at all levels of government (national, state, and local) and can declare these laws or acts to be unconstitutional—that is, beyond the limits set by the federal Constitution.

Throughout recent history, justices of the Supreme Court have varied in their outlook on the use of their powers of judicial review. Two clear tendencies have emerged: one group of justices has appeared to contain judicial activists and another group has stressed judicial restraint.

Those who take the position that judges should be very reluctant to declare laws or official behavior to be unconstitutional argue that judges are not elected and so there must be a special presumption of constitutionality when dealing with

[8] *Congressional Quarterly Weekly Report* (June 25, 1971), p. 1391.

acts of a popularly elected legislature, whether it be Congress, state legislatures, or city councils. Judges should not make policy but should instead interpret the law as precisely as possible.

Those who argue for an activist position view judges as policy makers who should not shrink from the task. Judges are also part of the governing apparatus and should act on the basis of their understanding of the nature of the political system and the demands of democratic values.

Activism and restraint also appear in a political context. Glendon Schubert has summarized this view:

> We are now in a position to suggest a functional theory of judicial activism and restraint. The Court's basic policies remain stable over long periods of time, and changes that do occur reflect very fundamental changes in the general political system, of which the Court is a component part. The justices themselves are goal oriented, and their basic goals are the same as those that motivate other political actors. Majority rule among the justices determines the policy goals that the Court supports, and it is the underlying stability in the general political system that accounts for the continuity in the Court's policy-making, by assuring that the judicial majority will reflect the dominant majority in the larger political system. If Supreme Court justices were appointed for four-year terms in phase with the presidential electoral cycle, then it could be anticipated that there would be considerably less stability in the Court's policy-making, because Court majorities would be more responsive to the short-run waves than to the long-run currents of political change. Under our constitutional system, it is precisely at the times of major realignment in the political party system that the Supreme Court is most likely to become involved in conspicuous and dramatic conflict with the Presidency and the Congress, because the majority of the justices then represent the minority in the new political realignment.[9]

In short, the Court appears to be dominated by activists when its policy views differ from those of other political actors. And it appears to be dominated by those who believe in restraint when there are a minimum of tensions between the

[9] Glendon Schubert, *op. cit.*, p. 153.

views of the members of the Court and the views of other political actors, including the president and Congress.

A critical concept that allows the Court substantial leeway in stressing either restraint or activism is that of the political question. The Court can declare an issue to be a political question—that is, one that must be settled by the other, more political, organs of government. The Court has used this declaration to avoid questions thought to be too hot to handle or questions on which, even if it made a decision, the Court would have no hope of enforcement of the decision. For a number of years, for example, the Court avoided suits involving the apportionment and districting of legislative districts, both for Congress and for state legislatures. These issues were declared to be political ones that the Court said it could not decide. Then in the 1960s, because new justices held different values, the Court changed its mind and involved itself heavily in the undoubtedly political questions of redistricting and reapportionment.

Even the most activist justice, however, would be likely to welcome the cover of the political question doctrine on some matters. For example, it was hard to imagine any justice willingly attempting to decide the constitutionality of the Vietnam War. Regardless of the decision, the Court would have been unable to enforce it; and regardless of the decision, the Court would have alienated large numbers of people. Although the Court is not in business to retain its popularity, most justices realize that courting extreme unpopularity is running a large risk in terms of respect for the Court and, therefore, its effectiveness in the political system. If the president, Congress, and state and local officials, supported by the public, have low respect for the Court's decisions and decide to ignore or at least circumvent them, there is little the Court can do. The ultimate sanction is, of course, the possibility that Congress may change the appellate jurisdiction of the Court, simply removing controversial matters from the Court's purview. But even short of this ultimate sanction there are other limits on the Court: constitutional amendments, laws in specific subject matters areas, executive orders and other presidential actions, nonconformity by lower courts, open defiance by state and local officials, and so on. Thus, the Court cannot proceed oblivious to public opinion or the opinion of other officials at all levels of government.

THE DOCTRINAL IMPACT OF THE COURT

The Supreme Court has, in general, been remarkably bold. On the face it should not be very powerful. It is not large and has no executive apparatus unless the executive branch willingly cooperates. Yet, it has embedded itself, through its announced decisions, in the political life of the nation, and most governmental units obey most of its decisions most of the time.

The court has involved itself in three basic kinds of relationships: (1) relations between differing governmental units, (2) relations between private citizens, and (3) relations between governmental units and private citizens. Although decisions stemming from the first and second relationships have been notable, by far the most important constitutional decisions have been generated from the third relationship.

RELATIONS BETWEEN GOVERNMENTAL UNITS

Before 1937 the Court spent a great deal of time worrying about cases involving questions of what the federal government could do in the economic realm and what was reserved to state and local units of government. In recent years the Court has basically followed the line that whatever the national government wants to do cannot be stopped solely on the grounds that it involves powers reserved to state and local governments.

The Court also occasionally gets involved in the relations between president and Congress. Ordinarily, such matters would be declared political questions and the Court would therefore remove itself from a touchy situation. However, the Court does act on occasion. For example, in 1952 it declared the seizure of the steel mills of the nation by President Harry Truman to be unconstitutional because of an implication the Court read into congressional behavior that Congress did not want the president to have the power of seizure. Even with such a strained line of reasoning (and three dissenting justices) the president immediately acquiesced and returned the mills to their private owners.

Relations between Private Citizens

In relations that on their face appear to be wholly private, the Court has been willing to rule some kinds of agreements unconstitutional on the grounds that the power of the government (usually state or local) is needed for purposes of enforcing the agreements. For example, in 1948 the Court ruled that so-called restrictive covenants contained in real-estate deeds could not be enforced in courts. These covenants typically prevented the owner of a house or lot from selling his property to anyone other than whites. The Court held that no court could enforce this agreement through supporting a suit against a person violating the covenant. Thus, the covenant could still be included in deeds, but it would represent words without legal force.

Other examples of private parties that become tinged with public character include a labor union certified by the government as an official bargaining agent, a nominally private library that receives some public support, and a restaurant owner leasing government property. None of these individuals or groups of individuals can engage in discriminatory practices, especially on the basis of race. In general, the Court is moving toward a doctrine in which virtually any racial discrimination is likely to involve state action and therefore will be held unconstitutional. Typically, the Court has not made (and probably will not make) such a sweeping pronouncement. On the other hand, an unbroken string of cases point in this direction.

Relations between Governmental Units and Private Citizens

The most important areas of constitutional decision making by the Court is that covering relations between governmental units (federal, state, and local) and private citizens. This is the area in which individual rights are most clearly at stake, and it is the area in which the Court has been at its boldest, particularly in the last few decades.

211

In the realm of criminal justice the Court has gradually extended all of the guarantees for defendants in federal trials to defendants in state trials. Thus, no defendant can be put in a position of incriminating himself, he must be able to confront the witnesses against him, he must have access to legal counsel at all stages of criminal proceedings, and evidence obtained through unconstitutional searches and seizures cannot be admitted as evidence in trials.

In the area of protecting free speech and press the Court has never decreed that any kind of speech or printed or filmed material is protected. It has consistently recognized the right of the government to prohibit certain kinds of expression: incitement to violence and hard-core pornography, for example. The Court leans over backward to define expressions of opinion as being protected by the Constitution but occasionally does rule in favor of a governmental action limiting expression.

A continuing set of issues before the Court revolves around the question of separation of church and state. For example, the Court in the 1960s ruled unconstitutional the practice of giving prayers, even on a voluntary basis, in public schools.

In the area of legislative apportionment and districting the Court ruled, in a series of cases, that districts for both houses of state legislatures and for the U.S. House have to be based on a one-man, one-vote principal.

Civil rights have been a continuing concern of the Court, which has ruled segregation in education and in virtually any public facility (swimming pools, golf courses, transportation) to be unconstitutional. It has also been very skeptical of local plans, particularly in the field of education, that appear to be designed to permit evasion of orders to desegregate meaningfully.

The Impact of the Court on Society

Supreme Court decisions are not usually self-executing. They depend on compliance from court of appeals judges, federal district judges, and a variety of state and local judges. In many cases they depend on compliance from federal, state, and local bureaucrats. They may require compliance from legislators in

Congress, state legislatures, and city councils. They may require compliance from large masses of private citizens. All of these groups and individuals vary in their willingness to comply with specific decisions depending on what is at stake. In general, noncompliance increases as unpopular decisions aggregate in a specific subject matter area, when there are economic components to a decision, when procedural rather than substantive matters are at stake, when the guidelines for enforcement and the meaning of the decision are murky, when a decision is not unanimous, and when the decision is broad in geographical scope and affects a large number of people or levels of government or both.[10] However, even within these limits, federal courts have made a major contribution to the shaping of American public policy.

[10] Stephen L. Wasby, *The Impact of the United States Supreme Court: Some Perspectives* (Homewood, Ill.: Dorsey Press, 1970).

PART 4

The Dynamics of Policy Response

CHAPTER 10

The Making of
Public Policy

The production of policy responses by the American national government is, as should be obvious by now, extremely complex. There are biases built into the system—biases in favor of slow, deliberate action on a limited range of problems instead of rapid, wide-ranging action on a great number of problems simultaneously and biases that favor the interests of the more privileged in society rather than the less privileged. Yet, neither set of biases absolutely precludes rapid, wide-ranging action or action deliberately aimed at greater equality for the less privileged. Thus, the system has some constraints; it also has substantial flexibility.

In presenting an overview of policy making in the American national government, several interesting generalizations seem useful in explaining how the system operates. These generalizations will be listed here and discussed in the remainder of this concluding chapter.

1. Most policies tend to be handled in a patterned, routine fashion.

217

2. This patterning and routinization is in part expressed through a reasonably stable set of relations between various publics (both mass and specialized), officials of institutions, and policy responses.

3. The patterning and routinization is also expressed in part through the existence of a chronological sequence of policy activity that tends to repeat itself (at different speeds) regardless of the subject matter area being acted on.

4. The stakes in a given decision help determine the decision-making pattern surrounding that decision and also help allocate relative degrees of influence to different institutional participants.

5. The normal tendency of the system to fragmentation, specialization, and incrementalization can be overcome under specific conditions.

Publics, Officials, and Policies

Most policies tend to be handled in a patterned, routine fashion. This is in part because there are great elements of stability built into the American political system. One study [1] has identified the following sources of great stability in all American policy making: (1) stable party identification and voting allegiances (Chapters 3 and 4 of this volume also make this point); (2) the strong tendency for all budget decisions to be incremental—adding or subtracting only small amounts of money; (3) the heavy reliance by legislators on executive requests for budgets—Congress typically makes only incremental changes in those requests; (4) the reliance by American policy makers on "the spending-service cliché"—"a routine which equates levels of expenditure with levels of service-output" [2]; and (5) the tendency of various American governments to copy each other's policies and procedures, which means

[1] Ira Sharkansky, *The Routines of Politics* (New York: Van Nostrand Reinhold, 1970).
[2] *Ibid*. p. 106.

that innovations soon become commonplaces and widely accepted.

The same study also indicates that there are factors that are constantly at work to stimulate change in the routines of decision making (although they will not necessarily change the policy responses themselves). Both political parties and interest groups are portrayed as making decisions by other means than the use of patterned routines.

Not only are the decision-making routines themselves a major factor in producing stable lines of policy decision, but the relationships between the various actors in the political system also tend to remain reasonably stable and contribute to predictable policy statements and actions.

The basic relationship between the major political actors (publics—both mass and specialized—and governmental officials in all branches) and policy statements and actions is simply portrayed in Figure 10–1.

This figure indicates that officials and publics interact before officials produce policy. Thus, officials have a direct impact on the nature of policy, although they certainly do not determine all of it without reference to anyone or anything else. Publics also have an impact on policy, but this impact is mediated through officials. This simple statement about the basic relationships does not assume that *all* aspects of policy come from either the public or from officials or from a combination of them, but it does assume that publics and officials are important in determining some important aspects of policy. However, it is also true that forces and events in both the natural and social environment also have important impacts

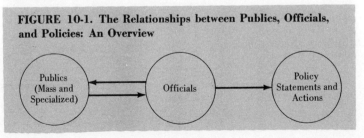

FIGURE 10-1. The Relationships between Publics, Officials, and Policies: An Overview

219

on policy responses, including policy results (that is, what happens in a society following policy statements and actions).

A more elaborate version of the simple notions contained in Figure 10–1 is presented in Figure 10–2. This figure suggests that all levels of the public interact with all types of officials, that all types of officials interact with each other, and that all types of officials help produce policy statements and actions. (Naturally, these policy statements and actions also have links to what happens in society—policy results—and also have influence on what publics and officials believe and do subsequently, but for the sake of simplicity, these relationships are omitted from the figure.) There are also important relationships within the various circles—different interest groups in-

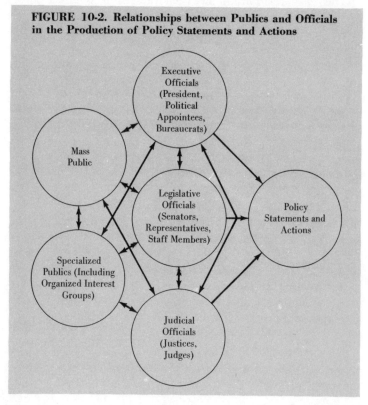

FIGURE 10-2. Relationships between Publics and Officials in the Production of Policy Statements and Actions

teract, bureaucrats interact with each other and with the president and his appointees, individual members of Congress interact with each other, and so on.

The Policy Process

There are a number of recurring subprocesses and stages in the production of policy statements and actions with predictable patterns of influence being wielded by identifiable participants.

Policy statements and actions tend to emerge in four different subprocesses, each of which is characterized by five recurring stages. Table 10–1 summarizes the subprocesses and stages in policy-statement and action development in the American national government. Obviously, not all policies go through all stages, and sometimes the chronological order varies, but the scheme is presented as representing a genuinely useful analytical model.

Formulation means the development of a preferred choice. Legitimation means the ratification, amendment, or rejection of that choice in its details. Note that what has been called policy administration—that is, the implementation of program decisions —is included here in the subprocess by which policy actions are legitimated.

The five stages of the policy process tend to repeat themselves in each of the four subprocesses:

1. The stage of *information collection* is one in which a problem is identified for government action and the search for information on the scope of the problem and on possible approaches to dealing with it is undertaken. All relevant information on either the problem or possible solution is never available or collected. The choice of the subjects on which information is collected is extremely important—this choice in effect eliminates some subjects from the government's agenda and puts others on it.

2. The stage of *information dissemination* is one in which those who have collected the information on the problem and

221

TABLE 10-1. The Policy Process in the National Government

Product	Subprocess (with Example)	Stages
Policy Statements	Formulation (e.g., requesting authorizing legislation or a major amendment to existing authorizing statutes)	Information Collection Information Dissemination Alternative Development and Selection Advocacy Preferred Policy Choice
	Legitimation (e.g., passing authorizing legislation or a major amendment to existing authorizing statutes)	Information Collection Information Dissemination Alternative Development and Selection Advocacy Policy Decision
Policy Actions	Formulation (e.g., requesting appropriations; formulating specific guidelines for implementing a program)	Information Collection Information Dissemination Alternative Development and Selection Advocacy Preferred Program Choice
	Legitimation (e.g., passing appropriations legislation; operating a program according to specified guidelines)	Information Collection Information Dissemination Alternative Development and Selection Advocacy Program Decision

possible solutions pass it along to those with more formal power to make decisions. Usually, the information is condensed before being passed on. Often it is condensed to serve the particular goals of those doing the disseminating.

3. *Alternative development and selection* is a third important stage in the policy process. At this stage solutions are the specific focus. Usually, several solutions are considered. Some alternatives are dropped from consideration; some are kept.

4. The fourth important stage is *advocacy*. The partisans of the remaining solutions thought to be feasible make their respective cases where they think they will do the most good. Occasionally, most or all of the advocates will agree on one solution and unite in pushing it. Usually, two or more alternatives receive serious and meaningful and potentially successful advocacy.

5. The fifth stage represents a decision stage either in terms of what is asked for (*preferred choice*) or in terms of what is granted or done (*decision*). In the subprocesses that lead to policy statements, the fifth stage is a *preferred policy choice* in the formulation subprocess and *policy decision* in the legitimation subprocess. In the subprocesses that lead to policy actions, programs are usually what is at stake. Programs constitute the units of action through which policy action emerges. Thus, the fifth stage in the formulation subprocess is labeled *preferred program choice*, and the fifth stage in the legitimation subprocess is labeled *program decision*.

Preferred program choices and program decisions sometimes radically alter the intent of the policy statement upon which they are supposedly based. At other times there is greater congruence. Program decisions are what determine governmental policy action. Implementers usually assume they know how their decisions will affect policy results in society, but in fact results often seem largely independent of action. Even in the most favorable circumstances the correspondence between expected results and actual results is rarely one-to-one.

Table 10–2 summarizes a series of judgments about relative influence by the major institutional participants at the different stages. A single *x* signifies some influence, a double *x* signifies

TABLE 10-2. Relative Institutional Influences in the Policy Process in the American National Government

Stage	Institutional Participant			
	Congress	Presidency	Bureaucracy	Interest Groups
Information Collection	x	x	xxx	x
Information Dissemination	x	x	xxx	x
Alternative Development and Selection	xx	xx	xx	x
Advocacy	xx	xxx	x	x
Policy Choices and Decisions	xxx	xxx	—	—
Program Choices and Decisions	x	x	xxx	xx

considerable influence, and a triple *x* signifies primary influence. This table is based both on impressionistic judgments and on a reading of empirical studies.

The table suggests several conclusions:

1. The bureaucracy appears dominant at the beginning of the process and again at the end of the process. It is preeminent in the information-collection and information-dissemination stages no matter what subprocess is involved. This means that the bureaucracy is basically responsible for choosing what topics are included on the agenda of government. Naturally, the agenda choice is influenced by events in society, but within the government the bureaucracy is dominant in determining the nature of what gets seriously considered, particularly on matters that do not have high enough public visibility to make them evident to the president or to large numbers of senators and representatives. Not only does the bureaucracy dominate the decision on what subjects warrant serious information collection, but the bureaucracy is also responsible for the initial pruning of the collected information so that it can be disseminated in manageable form and amounts. Thus, the bureaucrats make critical choices that influence later decisions by

highlighting some information and minimizing or deleting other information.

Once the process arrives at the level of program choices and decisions, the bureaucracy again is the most influential institutional participant. It is bureaucrats who are responsible for framing the programmatic choices and implementing the programmatic decisions, although it should also be noted that interest groups become relatively important in influencing the precise shape of programs, whereas at the information-collection and dissemination stages the interest groups have only occasional influence.

2. In the selection and development of alternatives the bureaucrats are also important, but at this stage Congress and the presidency become centrally influential actors. At this point genuine competition over ideas and between and within instititutions is typical.

3. The advocacy stage is the one in which the president can be dominant, if he so chooses. He will not always get his way but the great attention that he commands when he makes a concerted effort to advocate a specific alternative gives him a very large advantage. Congress, through individual members and groups of members, can also be quite influential during the advocacy stage.

4. Congress and the president are the decision makers in terms of policy choices and decisions since most such choices and decisions require legislation. The newspapers and a large part of political-science writing focus on the policy-choice and decision stage exclusively. This gives a mistaken impression about the overall importance of Congress and the president in relation to the bureaucracy. When seen in perspective, it is fair to say that Congress and the president dominate this stage, but they are acting on the basis of information and alternatives that have come in large part from the civil servants in the government.

5. Interest groups play a relatively minor role in all stages except program choices and decisions. But, as has been indicated throughout this volume, such detailed decisions are precisely where interest groups can gain the most for their mem-

bers with the least amount of public attention or attention even from Congress as a whole (as differentiated from individual subcommittees) or the presidency.

Substance and Process

What is at stake in any given policy discussion helps structure the decision-making pattern surrounding that policy area. That is, if an individual knows how the political actors view what they are doing in making specific policy decisions, then he can predict such things as what kinds of coalitions will form, where the final decision will be made in the political system, and where the decision will be implemented. One provocative attempt to make such predictions has come from Theodore Lowi, and what follows is an adaptation of his ideas.[3]

Domestic policy can be classified into one of three different categories: distributive, regulative, and redistributive. Distributive policies are those in which the government attempts to stimulate private activity that private citizens or groups would presumably not undertake otherwise. A distributive policy is basically a subsidy. These policies are perceived as distributing resources from a seemingly unlimited pool—that is, a winners-and-losers syndrome is not present in the competition for subsidy, except in the narrow sense of, for example, one company getting a government contract at the expense of another company. However, for the most part the actors involved in the discussion over a given subsidy do not perceive themselves to be engaged in taking away support from other enterprises, and those other enterprises do not perceive themselves to be threatened by the existence of still other subsidies. The cotton farmer, the wheat farmer, the ship owner, and the builder of components for submarines can all live peacefully with each other and with each other's subsidies, because all assume that the resource pool is adequate to meet most of their needs.

[3] Theodore Lowi, "Distribution, Regulation, Redistribution: The Functions of Government," in Randall B. Ripley, *Public Policies and Their Politics* (New York: Norton, 1966).

Regulatory policies are those in which the government sets certain conditions under which various private activities may or may not take place. Implementation of regulatory policies is on a case-by-case basis, but some of the decisions have wider application. In addition, some regulation takes place by the granting of licenses and franchises (for example, television channels are allocated by the Federal Communications Commission); this means that winners and losers perceive themselves as such because they directly compete for a visibly limited resource.

Redistributive policies are those in which the government takes action that is perceived to be to the benefit of one large collection of people (for example, a social class or a race) and to be at the expense of another large collection of people. Those receiving the benefits can perceive themselves as winners, while those from whom resources are taken to be redistributed think of themselves as the losers.

The government uses a variety of specific techniques as it engages in each of these kinds of activity.[4] Some of the *subsidizing techniques* include research grants, grants-in-aid, price supports, procurement of materials, and taxation. Research grants are currently especially important in the space field and in scientific development in general. Grants-in-aid are used to subsidize activity in the fields of education, mental health, hospital construction, and airport construction, among others. Price supports have provided billions of dollars of subsidy to the American farmer. Many more billions are spent on procuring the equipment that the government needs. The magnitude of expenditure is especially large in the building of a vast military arsenal to meet the varied demands of modern defense. Taxes can be used to subsidize by granting exemptions and special tax rates to certain types of persons, corporations, or activities.

Specific regulatory techniques are numerous. Some of the more important ones at the present time include dissolution of private arrangements pricing prohibitions, judicial and quasi-

---

[4] This discussion is adapted from the introduction to Randall B. Ripley, *op. cit.*

judicial proceedings, public appeals (especially by the president), certificates of convenience, necessity, or safety, and taxation.

The government has been interested in dissolving private arrangements that run counter to the public interest since the Sherman Antitrust Act of 1890. Since then, the number and variety of prohibited arrangements have multiplied. Certain kinds of price policies are prohibited and others are limited under various statutes. The government can go to court to request abatement of certain practices—air and water pollution of a specific description, for example. The regulatory commissions themselves act in part like courts, and thus a cease-and-desist order from the Federal Trade Commission comes only after a hearing in which the parties accused of unlawful business practices participate. Public appeals by the president have a regulatory impact. If a president asks for stable prices or stable wages in certain industries, his words, particularly if backed by a willingness to use the prestige and power of his office, are an attempt to prescribe conditions under which private activity can take place.

Many government agencies issue certificates allowing certain kinds of activity to proceed because given conditions have been met. The Federal Aviation Agency, for example, must certify that aircraft are safe before they can fly on commercial routes. Taxation can also be used to regulate private activity. High taxes on certain kinds of goods deemed to be socially harmful can in effect keep their production low or eliminate it altogether.

Taxation is the traditional government technique for accomplishing redistribution of resources. In recent years new fiscal and monetary techniques for reducing social imbalance and inequality have been developed. The fiscal agencies of the government operate using their powers over interest rates, discount rates, and bank reserve requirements for redistributive ends. Insurance schemes—such as Social Security and Medicare—have definite redistributive ends. Apparently regulatory measures such as wage-and-hours laws can have a redistributive impact. In the labor and civil-rights fields the government has developed a whole range of redistributive techniques—including the mediation of labor disputes and numerous ways of causing the government's persuasive and financial powers in the cause of equal rights for all citizens.

Table 10–3 summarizes a range of characteristics that are associated with each of the types of policy. This table seeks to summarize the answer to the question "What can be predicted from knowing that a policy falls into a particular category?"

Distributive policies involve individual units (either persons or corporations) as the basic political units. These units all wish to share in the subsidies being offered by government, and so they either support each other's claim to subsidy (log-rolling) or they simply do not pay any attention, positive or negative, to others' claims, because they are not viewed as competing (mutual noninterference with uncommon interests). Decisions tend to be made by small groups of individuals in any given subject matter field (for example, a bureau chief, lobbyist for a corporation, and subcommittee chairman), and these same groups of individuals persist for long periods of time, thus giving stability to the underlying structure of interests in the subject-matter fields in the distributive arenas. Formal decisions tend to be made either at the committee or subcommittee level within Congress or at the bureau level within the executive branch. Policies are implemented at the bureau level of executive agencies (but specific changes in implementation procedures and policies are also checked out with the other members of the subsystem in Congress and the private sector).

Regulatory policies involve groups, not always formally organized, as the basic political units. These groups typically form coalitions that work for the avoidance of outside regulation of their own activities (they may be willing to propose self-regulation) or for the regulation of competing interests that would work to their own advantage. There are many competing centers of power in this arena. The structure is unstable because coalitions keep forming, dissolving, and reforming along different lines as interests change. The most important decisions tend to get made on the floor of the House and Senate

TABLE 10-3. Arenas and Political Relationships: A Diagrammatic Survey

Arena	Primary Political Unit	Relation Among Units	Power Structure	Stability of Structure	Primary Decisional Locus	Implementation
Distribution	Individual, firm, corporation	Logrolling, mutual noninterference, uncommon interests	Nonconflictual elite with support groups	Stable	Congressional committee and/or agency	Agency centralized to primary functional unit ("bureau")
Regulation	Group	"The coalition," shared subject-matter interest, bargaining	Pluralistic, multicentered, theory of balance	Unstable	Congress, in classic role	Agency decentralized from center by "delegation," mixed control
Redistribution	Association	The "peak association," class, ideology	Conflictual elite, i.e., elite and counterelite	Stable	Executive and "peak associations"	Agency centralized toward top (above "bureau"), elaborate standards

Source: This table appeared in Theodore Lowi, "Distribution, Regulation, Redistribution: The Functions of Government," in Randall B. Ripley, ed., *Public Policies and their Politics* (New York: Norton, 1966), p. 39.

230

(Congress, in its classic role). Implementation of the policies is effected in a partially decentralized, partially centralized mode in the relevant parts of the executive branch.

Redistributive policies involve associations that are formally organized and typically large and that represent large numbers of people or large interests. So-called peak associations (that is, associations of associations) are important in this arena, and they become identified with social classes and with ideologies. Typically, elites representing conflicting interests are in direct conflict in policies in this area (for example, labor versus management; middle-class suburban whites versus ghetto blacks). The structure is stable in that the same competing elites appear again and again on related issues. The most important decisions are made in the executive branch at the higher levels (the president and his appointees) and in the peak associations themselves; implementation takes place at a relatively high level of the executive branch.

Inaction, Action, and Innovation

Final important questions about the American national government are what produces relatively high levels of action (some of it of the innovative variety) and what produces relatively low levels of action? There is no way of predicting specific substantive solutions to problems that emerge (in part, because there is no solid way of predicting which problems will be put on the agenda of government). However, several general statements can be made about conditions that tend to produce great levels of activity and innovation. First, certain institutional relationships are particularly critical in determining the level of activity. Second, innovation in the bureaucracy tends to require an infusion of democracy in a hierarchical system; innovation stemming from Congress tends to require an infusion of autocracy in a pluralistic system. Third, leadership is the key to overcoming the natural results of complexity, fragmentation, and incrementalism present in the American national government.

231

INSTITUTIONAL RELATIONSHIPS

The American national government is complex and fragmented; incremental change in small doses is the natural result of complexity and fragmentation. Little change occurs in any given status quo unless certain key institutions are in agreement and the channels of communications between those institutions are in good repair and being used. No one institution can produce policy by itself; necessarily, change (either innovative or noninnovative) involves agreements among institutions.

The core of the American national policy process is located in Congress and in the executive branch. Each of these institutional entities can be further reduced to key component parts. In Congress there are the party leaders, there are committee leaders (typically, committee and subcommittee chairmen and ranking minority members), and there are the rank-and-file members of the House and Senate. In the executive branch there is the president personally, there is the presidency collectively in the form of the Executive Office of the President and the presidential appointees, and there are the civil servants throughout all of the agencies. Every one of these six component parts of the central policy-making system has relations with every other component part, but some of these relationships are more critical than others. These are portrayed in Figure 10–3.

Within the executive branch two relationships are critical—those of the president with Executive Office personnel and presidential appointees throughout the government, and those of Executive Office personnel and presidential appointees with civil servants throughout the government. The bureaucracy is so vast that the president cannot hope to have direct relationships with civil servants (except for a few career civil servants in the Executive Office and a few career ambassadors in the foreign service). Thus, the Executive Office personnel and presidential appointees scattered throughout the various departments and agencies take on special importance in serving as middlemen between the president and his programmatic ideas and the development of and implementation of those ideas in the bureaucracy.

FIGURE 10-3. Critical Relationships for Policy-Making in the National Government

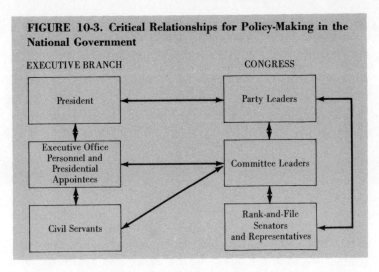

Three relationships are critical within Congress. If agreement and good relationships do not exist, then policy change is unlikely to occur. Committee leaders play something of a middleman role between party leaders and rank-and-file members, but party leaders also need direct ties to the rank and file; this is relatively easy to achieve in physical terms, given the limited size of the House and Senate. The committee leaders are typically the most important individuals in deciding what emerges from Congress in substantive terms. The party leaders make the strategic and tactical decisions about how best to get the work of the committee approved by the full House and Senate. The rank and file are approached by both committee leaders and party leaders in their respective spheres of expertise.

There are also three critical relationships between the executive branch and Congress; those between the president and the party leaders (largely on strategic and tactical matters), between the Executive Office personnel and presidential appointees and committee leaders (on substantive matters); and between civil servants in the executive branch and committee leaders in Congress (on substantive matters).

In short, to get very dramatic policy movement out of the

government, the eight relationships portrayed in Figure 10–3 must all be marked by a relatively high degree of mutual confidence and trust, and there must also be a relatively high degree of agreement on the nature of the problems facing society and the nature of proper solutions to those problems. These conditions are absent more than they are present, which helps to explain the normal posture of the government as moving very slowly on only a few problems at a time. Rapid movement on major issues occurs, and when it does it is unusual enough to be worth special notice.

CONDITIONS FOR INNOVATION WITHIN THE BUREAUCRACY AND CONGRESS

Normally the hierarchical structure of Congress is relatively flat—that is, there is considerable (although far from perfectly equal) dispersion of power in the House and Senate to individual members. Members can be influenced by party leaders and committee leaders, but they rarely respond to commands. The normal flat hierarchy allows every senator and representative to pursue his or her individual interests; there is no effective mechanism for aggregating these interests and focusing them on a given problem area in an innovative way. Short-term infusions of strong hierarchy (for example, strong party leaders) can provide the catalyst necessary to get Congress to move beyond the status quo.

On the other hand, the normal hierarchical structure of any piece of the executive branch (for example, a bureau) is relatively tall—that is, there are many formal levels of authority and superiors in a position to command subordinates, who in turn usually obey those commands. Under these conditions policy tends to vary only slightly from the status quo.

In the bureaucracy, tall hierarchies allow innovation only if they are activated by aggressive leadership, either from the bureau chief or from higher levels of the executive branch (including the president). Flat hierarchies in executive-branch bureaus allow creativity and communication across channels, as well as through channels, and even weak leadership at the top can be spurred on by grass-roots activity.

234

FIGURE 10-4. Policy Results of Distribution of Power in Congress and the Bureaucracy

		CONGRESS	
		Dispersed Power (Flat Hierarchy)	Centralized Power (Tall Hierarchy)
BUREAUS	Dispersed Power (Flat Hierarchy)	Frustrated Executive Branch Initiatives— Only incremental changes	High Probability of Innovative Policy Change
	Centralized Power (Tall Hierarchy)	Support of the Status Quo—Few changes (the "normal" situation)	Frustrated Congressional Initiatives— Only incremental changes

Figure 10–4 suggests the policy consequences of different mixes of congressional and bureaucratic hierarchical structures. It should be noted that it takes two unusual conditions for anything more than support of the status quo or incremental policy changes to result, namely dispersed power in bureaus and centralized power in Congress. As the figure shows, the government seems naturally to lean to slow, gradual change rather than to rapid, somewhat more dramatic change.

LEADERSHIP

Policy leadership in the American national government consists of the capacity on the part of an individual for influencing policy statements and actions in a desired direction through the use of available resources and the manipulation of constraining and facilitating conditions. By and large, in both the executive and legislative branches the leaders are those who hold the higher formal positions. Not all individuals in those positions possess the capacity described above and some individuals without formal positions have enough personal skills to become major influences, but it is still reasonable to expect more policy leadership from the formally defined leaders than from others.

Skillful leaders have emerged at various periods both in Congress and in the executive branch, and they will continue to

235

do so in the future. However, the American system of government is not run on the basis of strong personalities alone. A charismatic leader needs the proper setting, as well as his own skills, to succeed. An individual with somewhat lesser talents can be quite effective if the environmental and organizational setting is facilitative. This volume has tried to show how the production of public policy is not simply a matter of chance or idiosyncratic behavior by individuals but is, instead, related to a number of patterns and basic characteristics that can be analyzed systematically.

Governmental Responsiveness and Public Policy

There is a natural tendency for any government to become entrenched, inbred, and unresponsive to public needs and wants. What general statements can be made about the American national government in terms of its responsiveness? This question can be broken into three different questions that will allow some broad answers to be given.

First, does the American national government at least pay some attention to problems thought to be important by the American people? In general, the answer to this question is affirmative. Problems identified in public-opinion polls as being the most important are usually current objects of government attention. For example, polls in 1972 typically identified Vietnam, general economic conditions (including inflation), poverty and unemployment, and law and order as subjects of greatest concern to the largest proportion of the population. The federal government was at the same time working toward a peace settlement and cease-fire in Vietnam, administering a program of wage and price controls, administering a (diminished) war on poverty, and pursuing a stepped up program of providing aid to local law-enforcement agencies and concentrating particularly on an effort to stop trafficking in drugs. All of this activity, particularly that in relation to unemployment and poverty, was not necessarily of the most vigorous variety. However, at least some policy statements and actions were being made.

Second, does the government move in the direction desired by the public? In answering this question it must be recalled, of course, that on many issues the public is apathetic and ill-informed. And even on those issues in which there is wide-spread public interest there may be many and conflicting opinions. However, at least on a few issues, there does seem to be a genuine public majority in favor of a rather clear position.

The answer to this second question is mixed. Even when a majority seem to hold a clear, broad opinion—as for example, the seeming national consensus that pollution of air and water must be abated—government action is not unambiguous. Congress, for example, authorized a water-pollution program that would cost about eleven billion dollars. The president first vetoed the bill, and, when Congress passed the bill over his veto, he declared his intention simply to refuse to spend at least six billion dollars of the funds provided.

The record on seeking peace in Vietnam is also mixed. For a number of years the majority of the American public seemed to support the war effort, albeit usually half-heartedly. By 1968 or so, however, the tide of opinion definitely seemed to be turned in an antiwar direction. Some government actions—such as the suspension of the bombing of North Vietnam by President Johnson in the fall of 1968 (just before an election) and the announcement of serious peace negotiations by President Nixon in the fall of 1972 (just before another election)—were generally in accord with the trend of opinion. But other actions—such as the incursion into Cambodia by United States troops in the spring of 1970 (with elections a long way off)—ran counter to the trend of opinion (and antiwar students responded immediately to the Cambodian maneuver with violent demonstrations that resulted in the deaths of four students at Kent State University, among other things).

Third, are the channels of access to the system open? That is, can new points of view be heard and can new groups form that have a chance to present these views effectively? The answer here also seems to be a qualified yes. The qualification is that previously excluded groups in the society, having interests that are not effectively represented or holding views that are unpopular, must show considerable innovation in presenting their case. With aggressive leadership, however, that case can be made and heard. The civil-rights movement since the mid-1950s illustrates both the difficulties of being heard and the successes that can come when leaders such as Martin Luther King try new avenues, such as bus boycotts, sit-ins, and marches on Washington. Access is not automatic and easy for all groups, but neither is any sizable group absolutely prohibited from being heard. It is just easier for established groups from the more well-off segments of society to be heard than it is for previously voiceless groups from the less well-off segments of society.

In short, the responsiveness of the American government to public needs and wants provides no cause for unrestrained celebration of the perfection of the system. However, neither does it provide cause for unrelieved gloom and despair. As is so often true, a gray answer is less dramatic but more accurate than a black or white answer.

Govrnmental Policy Making in the 1970s

The American national government in the 1970s appears as if it will be operating in a very difficult setting. There will be a variety of changing circumstances that will create pressure for more and more policy statements and actions on a great many complex problems. At the same time, however, the changing circumstances will also allow the government to have less and and less assurance of achieving the desired policy results sought by those statements and actions.

Five kinds of circumstances appear to be particularly important. First, the institutions of government themselves will continue to change. For example, in the executive branch President Nixon announced shortly after his reelection in 1972 that he wanted to preside over a major overhaul and renovation of the executive branch. This presumably would include some major reallocation of functions and tasks, some major reduction in total federal employment, and some major changes in terms of leading personalities in the administration.

In his first term Nixon demonstrated his flair for such activity by successfully instituting a major reorganization of the Executive Office of the President: resulting principally in the creation of the Office of Management and Budget and the Domestic Council. In his second term Nixon wants to try his hand at reorganizing the entire executive branch.

Simultaneously, Nixon has announced his intention to revamp the policy views of the federal judiciary, especially the Supreme Court. As he began his second term in early 1973 Nixon had already appointed four of the nine Supreme Court's justices and it seemed likely that he would have several more appointments to make before his term expired.

Even Congress was moving slowly and hesitantly toward some institutional change. In the late 1960s and early 1970s the hold of seniority on committee appointments in both houses was weakened incrementally, at least in principle. The 1970s may well see additional changes—although gradual—come to Congress. In 1973, for example, the House created a Select Committee on Committees to review the entire committee structure of the House and recommend changes.

Second, the issues of the 1970s seem likely to provoke hot public debate between a variety of coalitions in a large number of visible issue areas. The question of foreign involvement generally (including continuing Indo-China questions), civil rights, ecological preservation versus economic expansion, defense spending for new weapons systems (including expensive aircraft and missile systems), law and order (the rights of the accused versus the rights of society), privacy (the rights of the individual versus the needs of the government to have reliable information), welfare (the work ethic versus the welfare ethic), and many other issues will all keep the pot of debate boiling and aggressive coalitions forming. The raucous debate between competing coalitions puts governmental institutions—themselves changing—under increased pressure.

Third, the partisan situation will continue to be unsettled. The Democrats are likely to retain at least nominal control of Congress, but presidential politics are far more clouded. Republicans are hoping that the elections of 1968 and 1972 are the harbingers of a new era of Republican dominance; Democrats are hoping that normal Democratic dominance will return in 1976 and succeeding years. Their hopes are enhanced by the Watergate troubles that will plague the Republican Party for at least several years. The supporters of Governor George Wallace of Alabama are hoping that he recovers his health and continues to pull the candidates of both major parties in a conservative direction, as he did in 1968.

Fourth, economic and social conditions seem likely to continue changing rapidly in the 1970s. Unemployment and the rate of inflation both seem determined to fluctuate. Migration patterns suggest the continuing isolation of the black masses in central cities. This not only affects housing integration adversely but also has implications for the relative integration or segregation of both public schools (especially with busing to achieve racial balance politically unpopular and on the wane) and jobs.

Fifth, the public is expressing less and less trust of government (and of other public institutions, as well). This makes the job of government even harder. A number of studies suggest a massive loss of trust and increase of cynicism or alienation in recent years. Even if the downward trend stops, stability would still mean a public wary of or even hostile to government. And one impact of Watergate almost surely will be to perpetuate a downward tend for a few years.

When asked whether the government in Washington could be trusted, seventy-seven percent of a national sample in 1964 replied "always" or "most of the time" and only twenty-two percent responded "some of the time." In 1970 only fifty-three percent said "always" or "most of the time" and forty-four percent said only "some of the time." In 1964 sixty-nine percent of the people thought that the people running the government knew what they were doing and only twenty-seven percent felt they did not know what they were doing. In 1970 these answers had changed to fifty-one percent who thought that the people running the government knew what they were doing and forty-four percent who did not think they knew what they were doing.[5]

A poll in 1972, when compared with a similar poll in 1966, found a dramatic loss of confidence in all institutional leaders —including the leaders of government institutions. Only about a quarter of the population in 1972 expressed a great deal of confidence in leaders of the U.S. Supreme Court (twenty-eight percent), the federal executive branch (twenty-seven percent), and Congress (twenty-one percent). Only six years earlier half of those polled had expressed confidence in members of the Supreme Court (fifty-one percent) and over four out of ten had expressed a great deal of confidence in leaders in the executive branch (forty-one percent) and in Congress (forty-two percent).[6]

A Last Word

We have seen how a large and fragmented government that normally makes policy statements and actions that represent only incremental changes from previous policy statements and actions works. More specifically, the impact of the political environment in which the government is set was first examined. This environment includes public opinion, political parties, voting and elections, and interest groups as its principal features. Second, the impact of the structure of national governmental institutions—the presidency, the bureaucracy, Congress, and federal courts—on policy was also examined. Finally, some general propositions were offered to explain what influences the government either to proceed in its normal way of

[5] Arthur H. Miller, "Political Issues and Trust in Government: 1964–1970." Paper prepared for delivery at the 1972 annual meeting of the American Political Science Association (Washington, D.C.: September 5–9).

[6] This is a Harris poll, reported in *The Chronicle of Higher Education*, vol. 7, no. 11 (December 4, 1972), pp. 1–2.

producing policy statements and actions or to discard part of its normal behavior and proceed in an extraordinary way.

This volume contains a large number of propositions about the policy behavior of the American national government. These propositions are meant to apply to all kinds of policies. Naturally, any given policy area is not likely to demonstrate the validity of all of the propositions offered. And, of course, there are likely to be exceptions to the general propositions in some specific instances. However, the framework of propositions offered in this volume is intended to provide a set of conceptual tools by which the reader can, in principle, interpret the significant features of any specific policy area and identify and understand the general patterns that are present.

Index

243